PINK
FLOYD
AND THE DARK SIDE
OF THE MOON

50 YEARS

Quarto.com

© 2023 Quarto Publishing Group USA Inc.
Text © 2023 Martin Popoff

First Published in 2023 by Motorbooks, an imprint of The Quarto Group,
100 Cummings Center, Suite 265-D, Beverly, MA 01915, USA
T (978) 282-9590 F (978) 283-2742

This book has not been prepared or approved by Pink Floyd, its individual members, or its representatives. This book is an unofficial publication.

Motorbooks titles are also available at discount for retail, wholesale, promotional, and bulk purchase. For details, contact the Special Sales Manager by email at specialsales@quarto.com or by mail at The Quarto Group, Attn: Special Sales Manager, 100 Cummings Center, Suite 265-D, Beverly, MA 01915, USA.

26 25 24 23   2 3 4 5

ISBN: 978-0-7603-7929-5
Digital edition published in 2023
eISBN: 978-0-7603-7930-1

Library of Congress Cataloging-in-Publication Data

Names: Popoff, Martin, 1963–author.
Title: Pink Floyd and the Dark Side of The Moon : 50 years / Martin Popoff.

Description: Beverly, MA : Motorbooks, 2023. | Includes index. | Summary:
  "Pink Floyd and The Dark Side of the Moon offers a generously
  illustrated deep dive into all aspects of one of the most popular rock
  albums of all time"—Provided by publisher.
Identifiers: LCCN 2022037148 | ISBN 9780760379295 | ISBN 9780760379301
  (ebook)
Subjects: LCSH: Pink Floyd (Musical group). Dark side of the moon. | Rock
  music—1971-1980—History and criticism.
Classification: LCC ML421.P6 P65 2023 | DDC 782.42166092/2—dc23
LC record available at https://lccn.loc.gov/2022037148

Design: Landers Miller Design
Page Layout: *tabula rasa* graphic design

Printed in China

PINK FLOYD

AND THE DARK SIDE OF THE MOON

50 YEARS

MARTIN POPOFF

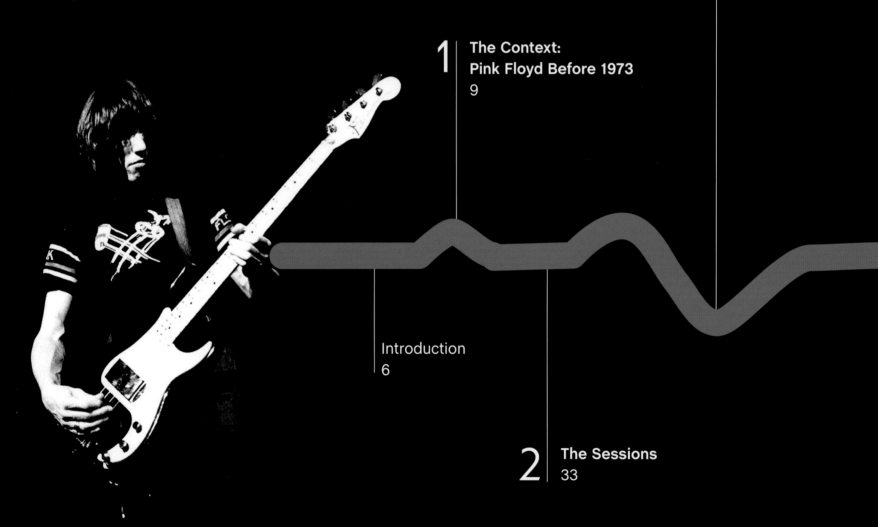

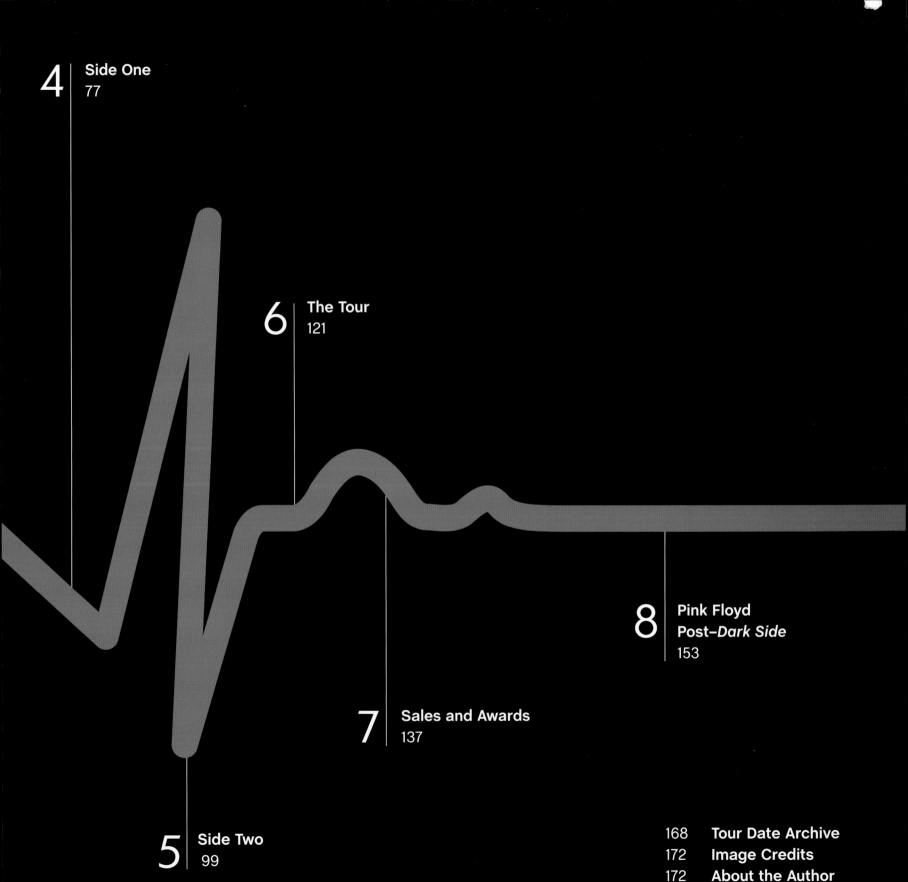

Introduction

Welcome one and all to what we hope you will find to be both a plush and intellectual approach to celebrating the fiftieth anniversary of Pink Floyd's landmark album, *The Dark Side of the Moon.*

Also, it is hoped that you will find the manner in which we've looked at this great record both fresh and useful, and that our partitioning into chapters and side excursions makes for easy and regular visits to the book if you choose not to read it like a regular book, from front to back.

The aim of this introduction is to ease you into the process, and certainly not to talk about *The Dark Side of the Moon*, because there is plenty of that to come. So yes, to go over a few points of process: first, I will regularly refer to the album as *Dark Side of the Moon* and not *The Dark Side of the Moon*. It just makes for a better read, and the shorter, technically incorrect version is widely the way folks discuss it. Second, a minor quibble along the same lines, but it must be addressed: "Breathe" and "Breathe (In the Air)" are used interchangeably throughout the book. There is no right answer, and indeed the first vinyl issue of the album calls the song "Breathe" in the gatefold (in two places) and "Breathe in the Air" on the record label! Third, we will provide ample background and context to the core story, leading up to the band's great feat of 1973, as well as a fair bit of detail as to what happened afterward with both the record's creators and the life of the album itself—in essence, this book serves also as the story of Pink Floyd, in abbreviated form, with all the detail emanating from one place.

Holding it all together will be a chronological frame, anchored in the middle by chapters in which we examine the songs themselves. The sidebars within those chapters consist of short profiles of Roger Waters, David Gilmour, Rick Wright, and Nick Mason themselves. We thought that would be a good place to situate these minibiographies, given two sides of music and four band members. So yes, little decisions like that were made along the way, with, I suppose, the chapters adhering closest to the chronology and the sidebars left to drift and dance a bit outside of it, as sidebars often do.

I must say that what made this project so satisfying to write is the timelessness of *Dark Side of the Moon*, beginning with its sonic qualities. Ever since my teen years in the late '70s, this theory has formed in my mind and then ossified over the decades: basically, that we have album production before *Dark Side of the Moon*, and we have album production after *Dark Side of the Moon*. The idea is that the production of this album—between what Alan Parsons, Peter James, Chris Thomas, and the band contributed—is optimal and perfect, and that from late 1973 forward, records can only sound different, not better. In other words, I've always had it stuck in my head that *Dark Side of the Moon* is the first album in history where any and all technological limitations were conquered; where not a single sound along the spectrum of the sonic palette was compromised by the machinery available in the day—quite the supposition, given that the guys were making this in the early '70s at Abbey Road.

Then there are the songs and the music, which represent a different kind of timelessness. Here again, the style of music Pink Floyd was writing at this point—say in contrast with *The Piper at the Gates of Dawn* and *A Saucerful of Secrets*, for example—is untethered to that time or even to a specific music genre, extinct or ongoing. Although, as pushback, one might debate that the bulk of today's music isn't made with guitars, bass, and drums, but rather with computers and computer sounds and whatever the word "synthesizer" means today. But I think that's as far as you can go. Which, sadly, is valid in this day and age: the very instruments used to create *Dark Side of the Moon* sometimes seem antique, as do the methods of wrestling them down onto . . . tape.

Representing a third layer of timelessness is how massive the album became, and not even all at once, but vigorously and continually—even comically (see our sidebar about the Billboard 200)—over the decades, even living on as a giant past the CD age and the downloading age into the streaming age.

What I also find amusing is that this idea of timelessness associated with *The Dark Side of The Moon* was somewhat presaged through the fact that the tour for the album before it (and, in typical surreal creative Pink Floyd fashion, nobody even knows whether that means *Meddle* or *Obscured by Clouds*) was somehow, through sleight of hand, in fact the beginning of the *Dark Side of the Moon* tour.

And then, lo and behold, the guys mess with our minds further, when after touring the new album in the conventional sense in 1973, they begin the tour for *Wish You Were Here*, which, if you tilt it in the light, is actually still the *Dark Side of the Moon* tour. And then they don't actually tour *Wish You Were Here* once the record is out (confounding things even further, given the wild set list, maybe the band is also beginning the campaign for *Animals*).

But the collective laughing at convention from the band is unsettling. As we'll explore, *Dark Side of the Moon* represents a complicated, nuanced look at various forms of madness that germinates from within and then spreads to obsession, along with the madness of external pressures. And then there's the tragic (instructive, illustrative) madness that by this point is a buzzing, tormenting, headache-inducing part of the history of the band in the form of Syd Barrett. Alas, Syd's mental disintegration and necessary exile from the ranks had the band wondering how much the pressure of being in Pink Floyd might send their own heads around the bend.

And always looming over the subject of madness are even larger concepts such as time and purpose and death. Indeed, it's *Wish You Were Here* that seems to attract all the attention as the record about Syd because those themes are so simply stated there, but it's *Dark Side of the Moon* that has the Floyd reflecting on its past, present, and future most poignantly, and, in the realm of art and artistry, most triumphantly.

Not to denigrate the whole bloody lot of Pink Floyd's catalog before the band's eighth (!) album or after it, but I think most fans and students and scholars of the Floyd would designate *Dark Side of the Moon* as the band's masterpiece, even if it's not particularly that person's favorite (case in point, mine is *Animals*). Bottom line, by consensus, it's the band's best album.

We should never put too large a point on the following, but a clue to the album's greatness is the fact that it's one of the biggest-selling albums of all time at an estimated 45 million copies worldwide. What's more, people just haven't stopped talking about it, which, I suppose, well, here's another book talking about it—a lot.

In any case, have we justified the creation and existence of such a printed artefact in praise of *The Dark Side of the Moon*?

I hope so. But of course, consider this brief introduction only the opening salvo of that justification. Because, again, we're about to dig in, look at the record head-on but also from many angles, just like the prism on the front of it, refraction leading to reflection, in the ultimate hope that by the end of the book, you'll find yourself even more in love with the record than you were before, and indeed finding spots within it and across it that prompt you to reflect on what's happening within your own life. Ergo, maybe what we're going for is the establishment of *Dark Side of the Moon* as some sort of Hawkwind-styled Orgone Accumulator, a therapy machine of sorts, with this book serving as owner's manual, instructive illustrations included.

1 The Context
Pink Floyd Before 1973

"Remembering games and daisy chains and laughs"

Given the distinct and uncategorizable band that they would become, it's easy to forget that had they faded away in 1972, Pink Floyd would likely have been remembered more for being the first and best example of psychedelic rock, English style. To be sure, the band's early innovations, mostly at the hand of mercurial visionary Syd Barrett, would manifest in sophisticated, elliptical ways on the likes of *Meddle* and *Dark Side of the Moon*. But the band would create fearlessly past this invention phase we hear on the first two albums, and then also past a near cultural appropriation of what became known as Krautrock, as the guys—Roger Waters, David Gilmour, Rick Wright, and Nick Mason—fever-dreamed their way into the '70s. What is remarkable (and a credit to the public and even the music industry, particularly the band's label, Harvest) is that the band was allowed to live and even thrive on a modest level, making an astounding seven records before—if we are to be provocative about it—making music that was listenable! I'm being cheeky of course, but let's be truthful: Pink Floyd was allowed to live to fight another day (and then another) despite producing a lot of very difficult music along the way.

Pink Floyd, 1967. Left to right:
Nick Mason, Roger Waters,
Syd Barrett, Richard Wright

TOP & ABOVE: The band's namesakes, Pink Anderson and Floyd Council

ABOVE RIGHT: Pink Floyd before their gig at Gyllene Cirkeln (Golden Circle) in Stockholm, September 10, 1967, executed between a handful of Danish dates

OPPOSITE: Pink Floyd in 1967

Back to the beginning, the band came to their psych and prog rock bona fides the proper British way: whilst off-duty from their college studies. Roger and Nick were studying architecture while Syd had pitched up in London in 1962 to enroll in the Camberwell College of Arts. Pink Floyd formed in late 1964 when Syd joined Roger, a childhood friend, and Nick in the band along with guitarist Bob Klose.

A woodshedding period took place throughout 1965 when the band, at this point called the Tea Set, took up a residency at the Countdown Club in Kensington High Street, playing multiple sets and extending their selections through jamming and meandering solo excursions. In late 1965 the band became the Pink Floyd Sound, Syd coming up with the name on the spur of the moment when it was discovered that they were to be on a bill with another band called the Tea Set. Like the name ZZ Top, the new name was an homage to two bluesmen, in this case, singer/guitarists Pinkney Anderson and Floyd "Dipper Boy" Council.

The band's evolution from a sort of baby Rolling Stones into this new thing soon to be called psychedelia began in 1966, when their management company, Blackhill Enterprises, somewhat flush due to an inheritance, made sure that the guys had new equipment, instruments, and a light show, augmented by the projection of colored slides.

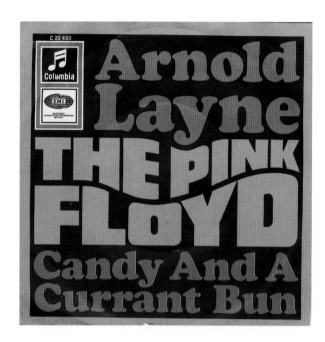

The German release of "Arnold Layne" (top) and the Japanese release (above) of the "See Emily Play"

Becoming notorious for their freaky shows at the UFO Club and bolstered by write-ups in the new underground press of the day, the band entered an equal partnership with their two managers, Peter Jenner and Andrew King, and inked a record deal with EMI.

Signing for an attractive £5,000 advance, Pink Floyd had their first record in the shops on March 10, 1967, a single pairing "Arnold Layne" with "Candy and a Currant Bun." "See Emily Play" b/w "Scarecrow" followed on June 16, as did the band's first TV appearances, on *Look of the Week* and *Top of the Pops*. It was at this point that Syd began to deteriorate due to an excessive use of LSD (for more on Syd, see sidebar, pages 26–27). However, the band's debut full-length album got made, with a wobbly Syd still the primary creative force, albeit for the last time.

The Piper at the Gates of Dawn, issued August 5, 1967, is pretty much the most famed and perfect psychedelic rock album to emerge out of London, every bit the cultural center for this genre as San Francisco. Aggressively druggy, the album opens with sampled spoken word, a future famed Floyd trope, which gives way to the swirling majesty of "Astronomy Domine," followed by the malevolent surf psych of "Lucifer Sam." The balance of the record introduces the lighter, pastoral, whimsical, and very delicate persona of Syd and his folkie psych musings (plus a bit of dancehall at times), which is marbled amid recurring doses of hard-ish rock psych and whacky sound effects. In other words, in composite, *The Piper at the Gates of Dawn* singlehandedly codified this new type of music, becoming the yardstick by which following examples would be measured. To be sure, full-length albums going to this place had already been issued, with credit going to the likes of *Pet Sounds*, *Revolver*, *The Psychedelic Sounds of the 13th Floor Elevators*, *Surrealistic Pillow*, and The Beatles once again with *Sgt. Pepper's Lonely Hearts Club Band*. But no one had leaned so hard into the unrelenting idea of psychedelia beyond garage or pop or blues roots at this juncture as Pink Floyd. Plus, they had the liquid light show to further underscore the effect.

Advertisement for the International Love-in Festival at Alexandra Palace, London, July 29, 1967. The lineup for this famous gig was Eric Burdon and the Animals, Pink Floyd, Brian Auger and the Trinity with Julie Driscoll, The Crazy World of Arthur Brown, The Creation, Tomorrow, Blossom Toes, Apostolic Intervention, and Sam Gopal Dream.

After several high-profile TV appearances and important live shows during which Syd appeared increasingly vacant, the band decided it needed another guitarist. Enter David Gilmour, who begins his life in the band as a sort of supporting brace to Syd live and, most significantly, on the second album, *A Saucerful of Secrets* (issued June 29, 1968). Barrett technically remained part of the team, appearing in the credits and writing and singing one song, "Jugband Blues," but it was Gilmour who played most of the guitar and even did a bit of singing, even if he received only one songwriting credit. And then famously, one day in January of '68, while en route to a gig, the band decided not to go 'round and collect Syd and that was it—he was out of the band. With Barrett went Blackhill, resulting in Steve O'Rourke becoming the band's manager, a post he would hold until his death from stroke in 2003.

Like the debut, *A Saucerful of Secrets* would be a chart success in the U.K., reaching #9 and spending eleven weeks on the local grid. The band would return to the U.S. for their first extensive tour there (a short trip with Syd previously had turned out to be a disaster) on a bill with Soft Machine and The Who. Both the tour and the second record represented business as usual, stylistically speaking (excepting the album's twelve-minute title track), although Roger now had to step up and write and sing more. It was a bit of an unspoken secret that these four Floyds were less creative than the departing one, but credit where credit is due, they grew into their roles quickly, particularly Roger.

ABOVE: London, 1967

OPPOSITE: Sleeves for the first two long players: *The Piper at the Gates of Dawn* (upper left) and *A Saucerful of Secrets* (lower right)

The soundtrack album *More* was mostly quite light but punctuated with a couple of hard rockers in "Ibiza Bar" and "Nile Song." It also represented the band's willingness to participate in experimental projects. The top shot is the *More* album cover and the bottom right shot is the Japanese single sleeve for "The Nile Song."

Hipgnosis employed the Droste effect for the sleeve art of *Ummagumma*.

Next, in June of '69, would come soundtrack album *More*, underappreciated and very much a Floyd album, mostly quite light and sensibly soundtrack-y in spots, but punctuated with a couple of hard rockers in "Ibiza Bar" and the popular "Nile Song." The album more so represented the band's willingness to participate in experimental projects, in this case film. *Ummagumma*, issued November 7, 1969, would represent the band's furthest reach into obscurity, featuring an egregiously psychedelic live set along with long solo compositions from the band over two fairly insufferable vinyl records.

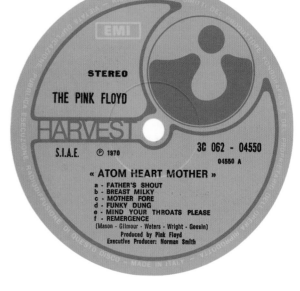

The sleeve of *Atom Heart Mother* came as something of a reaction to the band's desire not to be pigeonholed in a particular genre.

This was followed by *Atom Heart Mother*, released October 2, 1970. Despite trying their darnedest to get sacked, the band was still on Harvest, still selling records, and still playing to lots of freaks. But now they were also offering more commercial tracks in "Summer '68" and "Fat Old Sun." Elsewhere, especially across the side-long title track, Pink Floyd carved out a space for themselves few would dare visit, with songs as long as those constructed by fellow proggers, the difference being that very little seems to happen inside Pink Floyd's epics, and when it does, it happens quietly.

Still, it's remarkable that both *Ummagumma* and *Atom Heart Mother* have multiple gold and even platinum certifications around the world, which, again, is credit to the brave tastes of the record-buying public, who unfathomably pushed the latter to #1 in the U.K. charts. Granted, the awards wouldn't come for years, needing time and the band's ensuing massive fame to drag folks along, but along they came. (And on the topic of early Floyd records being somewhat hard to love, well, both Roger and David think *Atom Heart Mother* is crap.)

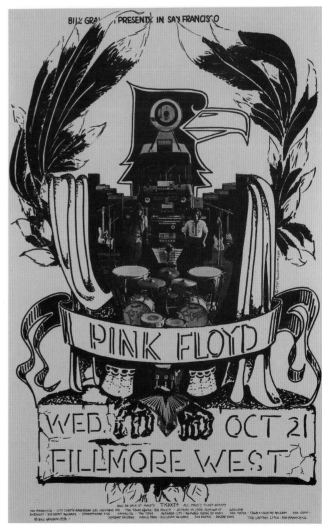

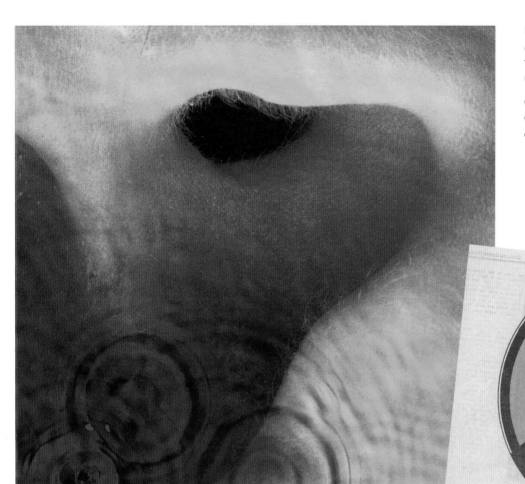

The new Pink Floyd album, MEDDLE,
is like throwing a party for your ears
when all your ears were expecting
were a few friends over for pinochle.

Available from Capitol

It was *Meddle*, issued November 5, 1971, that really found the band moving forward, not so much in concept, but with stronger material and better recordings. "One of These Days," "Fearless," and "Echoes," in composite, offered in proto form a portion of the various good ideas we'd hear on *The Dark Side of the Moon*. Also taking some time, *Meddle* would get all the way to double platinum in the U.S., with the record being the lone offering from that weird early-'70s tangle that sounds like the work of the same band that would deliver massive numbers across the rest of its catalog. And oddly (because Floyd can't do it any other way), it's opening instrumental "One of These Days" that lays out the plan best, with nightmarish sound effects, gnarly bass, grooving music, soundtrack drama . . . it seems clear that if they had found a way to put a vocal to it, the song might have been a smash hit.

The U.K. (above) and US (right)
sleeves of the hits package
Relics, released 1971

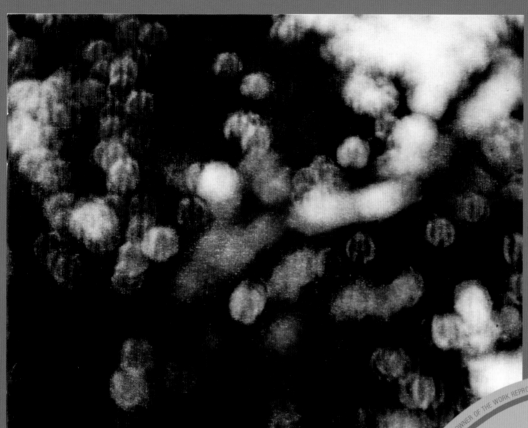

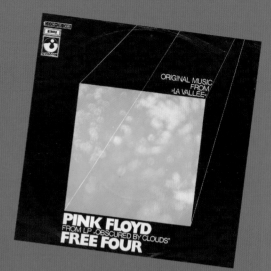

ORIGINAL MUSIC
FROM
"LA VALLEE"

PINK FLOYD
FROM LP "OBSCURED BY CLOUDS"
FREE FOUR

LC 1305

STEREO

ST 33

"The Gramophone Company Ltd."

HARVEST

GEMA Ⓟ 1972

1 C 072-05 054
A
Seite 1

OBSCURED BY CLOUDS
(Music From The Film "The Valley")
1. Obscured By Clouds (Waters/Gilmour) 3:03
2. When You're In (Waters/Gilmour/Mason/Wright) 2:21
3. Burning Bridges (Wright/Waters) 3:20
4. The Gold It's In The . . . (Waters/Gilmour) 3:01
5. Wots . . . Uh The Deal (Waters/Gilmour) 4:12
6. Mudmen (Wright/Gilmour) 4:58
PINK FLOYD
Prod. by Pink Floyd

PINK FLOYD

FREE FOUR

the gold it's in the...

沈着・緻密
濃厚・耽美
虚無・独善
狂気 そして…

雲の影 (フランス映画 The Valley より)

PINK FLOYD

雲の影／ホエン・ユー・アー・イン／炎の橋／ザ・ゴールド・イッツ・イン・ザ・／ウォッツ／花
まみれの男／大人への寓劇／フリー・フォア／スティ／アブソルートリー・カーテンズ／全10曲

EOP-80575　30=ステレオ　￥2,000　英国ハーヴェスト原盤

7月10日発売

Odeon RECORDS　東芝のオデオンレコード

ABOVE: Japanese advertisement for *Obscured by Clouds*. The album was recorded as the soundtrack to the 1972 French film *La Vallée*, but after a falling out with the studio, they named the album *Obscured by Clouds*.

OPPOSITE: The *Obscured by Clouds* album cover (top left) and British label (lower right), and the German (top right) and Italian (bottom left) releases of the "Free Four" single.

But wait, there's more. And like *More*, it came in the guise of another soundtrack album, *Obscured by Clouds*. Like *More*, the record is underappreciated and full of nice, conventional songs, with "Free Four" being particularly cheerful, making its release as a single sensible.

And there you have it, the "it" being quite a lot. Add "it" up and you've got a band arriving at *The Dark Side of the Moon* nearly eight years old and seven albums into their career. If you'd just heard those seven albums as a knowledgeable enough music fan, but without knowing any of the story, you'd reasonably arrive at the conclusion that this was a band that operated where there was no sunlight. But you'd be wrong. Despite the band's mostly inaccessible music, which, even when accessible could for the most part be described as sleepy, Pink Floyd was very actively touring the U.K., mainland Europe, and North America, playing huge festivals, appearing on loads of TV shows, doing soundtracks and double records and live records, and even making their own somewhat conceptual concert film. They'd even been to Japan twice by this point. In other words, the band had made for themselves a decent enough living while also turning in wildly eccentric and creative records that seemed to wilfully buck music trends.

This legacy of legendary (collective) individualism as well as sheer quantity (if not always quality) would put the band in good stead as they approached their next project, almost in a panic for new ideas but also in love with the intensity and challenge of being artists. In that light, *Dark Side of the Moon* would mark a moderate enough next step illustrative of the band's loopy thinking, but at the same time a huge leap in skills honed trying to capture strange sounds—in other words, evolution of concept, revolution of craft.

SYD BARRETT

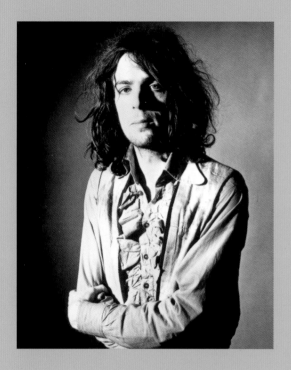

Roger Keith "Syd" Barrett was born January 6, 1946, in Cambridge, England. His tragic story—and quite rare, really, that of the acid casualty—would cast a pall over the early days of Pink Floyd. The ex-bandmates would periodically reflect on him in song as he slipped away and out of the music business—just as Floyd was making its ascendency.

A natural creative, in his childhood Syd drew and wrote and played piano, ukulele, banjo, and guitar. He was fifteen when his prominent doctor father died of cancer, bringing grief and drama to his previously sheltered life as part of a large family with five children. The result was escape into fairy tales and other literature and arts. Music took prominence for a spell before he

enrolled in the Camberwell College of Arts to train as a painter. By this point, having already been childhood friends with Roger Waters, he met David Gilmour and even played gigs with him, Gilmour on guitar and Barrett on bass. Soon, inspired by his love of The Beatles, Rolling Stones, and Bob Dylan (later came The Byrds and Love), Barrett was in the band that morphed through various names—the Abdads, the Screaming Abdads, Sigma 6, the Meggadeaths—to become Pink Floyd. Peter Jenner has said that "Syd was the only person Roger has ever really liked and looked up to" and David called him "a respected figure"—this was a good guy to have in your band.

Barrett took acid for the first time in the summer of 1965—actually with Storm Thorgerson, soon to found album cover design house Hipgnosis. There's no question that in the early days of the Floyd, it was Syd who had all the ideas and led the band, a fine-looking gentleman with elegant but modern fashion sense, appointing himself with confidence in interviews and thus making him the spokesman. But the acid, now a regular part of

his regimen, was having an effect. His musical tastes ran headlong into the experimental and his lyrics were attendant flights of fancy, acid trips on the page and yet anchored in a certain middle-class decorum in the English Romantic poetic tradition. As well, underscoring this idea that Syd was creativity personified, the exercise of painting was always mixed up with the poetry and then putting it to music.

Barrett's lasting artistic achievement would be *The Piper at the Gates of Dawn*. Affecting the direction of the album, EMI and engineer Norman Smith indulged the band's wilder tendencies but steered the project toward Syd's beautiful, origami-like vignettes and away from the live jamming, which wasn't winning converts the way Syd's pixie dust songs were. Uncommonly, the label allowed the band three months to make the record, somewhat influenced by how long The Beatles were taking with *Sgt. Pepper's*, working next door.

But Syd was deteriorating, evidenced by his showing up to TV appearances dressed in scruffy clothes when only recently he'd been the fashion horse in the band. The acid use was

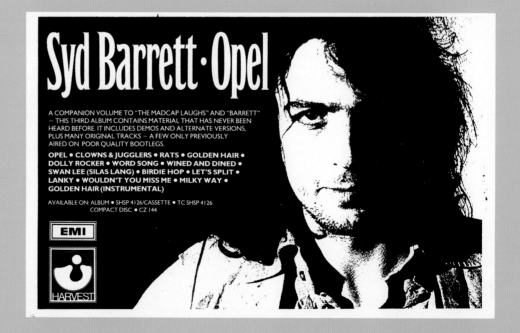

combining with the pressures of fame and the insistence that he write hit singles. He'd begun to dig in his heels with respect to taking the band's art even more extreme and not playing the games the music business required. Simultaneously he was methodically withdrawing from everything, from playing on demand, from answering when spoken to. As friend of the band June Boylan noted, Syd was eventually taking LSD three or four times a day, with Storm saying he was "into his 'orbiting' phase." His flat was an acid-themed drug den populated by people (and his two cats Pink and Floyd) tripping. Syd had decided he was going all-in. He was operating on himself.

The second album, *A Saucerful of Secrets*, went predictably, with Syd turning in very little and most of it off-the-cuff nonsense, resulting in a collection of songs without much Syd, but with shuddering memories from the band in retrospect, on how the record was a dark document of Syd having lost his mind, and now his place on the record and in the world.

Soon to be quietly exiled from Pink Floyd, Syd would be good for two harrowing solo albums essentially built up around anything coherent anybody could coax out of him. *The Madcap Laughs* and *Barrett*, both issued in

1970 and featuring Floyd members helping, didn't make Syd Barrett a star but rather marked the end of five years of making art from acid.

There would be periodic attempts by Peter Jenner, now managing Syd and not the Floyd, to coax Barrett back, with Syd living in and out of hotels, all the while forming loose collaborations with other underground London musicians that quickly went nowhere. The last full-court press took place in August 1974, with the plan being to get a third album out of Syd. Three days of sessions at Abbey Road resulted in eleven half-formed songs but nothing much of use.

To everyone's surprise, Barrett showed up at the studio in 1975 while Pink Floyd were mixing "Shine On You Crazy Diamond." Overweight and with his head and eyebrows shaved, he was barely recognized. He spent part of his visit brushing his teeth. In 1978, Syd moved back to Cambridge to live with his mother, then to London one last time and then back to Cambridge, walking the fifty miles to his last place of residence. Living again with his mother, he gardened, painted, took up photography, and otherwise lived the life of a recluse, dying at home on July 7, 2006, of pancreatic cancer.

Barrett's cautionary tale as one of rock's rare acid casualties would trouble the band. First, they would have to learn to make colorful words and music without their own Byron and Beardsley and Baudelaire, but then they'd take to heart that Syd was part of their history and appreciate that many of the pressures on him back in 1967 were now felt by a maturing Floyd. Syd's tale would thus directly and indirectly form the intellectual thrust of *Dark Side of the Moon*.

Reflecting as much, upon Syd's death, David Gilmour issued a statement, writing "We are very sad to say that Roger Keith Barrett—Syd—has passed away. Do find time to play some of Syd's songs and to remember him as the madcap genius who made us all smile with his wonderfully eccentric songs about bikes, gnomes, and scarecrows. His career was painfully short, yet he touched more people than he could ever know."

PROGRESSIVE ROCK

It's not a given that we have to go around calling Pink Floyd a "progressive rock" band, but it's pretty much agreed upon that if we're going to stick them in a box, that's the one. In that light, we'd like to describe what that term "progressive rock" encompasses as of *Dark Side of the Moon* and 1973, and how Pink Floyd runs with the pack and then also scampers off into the woods.

One way to view the genre's origins is as an outgrowth of psychedelic rock, which begat both prog and heavy metal, both styles beginning their long, gaudy lives in 1970. In crude terms, one might view Pink Floyd as proto-proggers through the likes of *More*

and *Ummagumma* and *Obscured by Clouds*, but there are truer examples of such prog progenitors. In fact, there's a whole movement called Krautrock (German bands cross-pollinating hard rock, jazz, and classical), but also the first Yes album in July 1969, the second Jethro Tull record, *Stand Up*, issued the following month, and fully five Moody Blues albums before 1970.

But progressive rock really becomes codified with the quite splashy arrival of key records from the likes of Yes, Genesis, Jethro Tull; Emerson, Lake & Palmer, and King Crimson in the early '70s. Yes comes on boldest, with *The Yes Album*, *Fragile*, and *Close to the Edge*, with the latter often considered the greatest prog album of all time. Genesis, with their second through fifth records, create a sound that is almost the median prog rock experience. For Jethro Tull, its hit record *Aqualung* and one-song concept record *Thick as a Brick*. ELP bring the drums and keyboard bombast, and all seven of their albums between 1970 and 1978 go gold. King

Crimson never had a bigger impact than they would with their debut record, *In the Court of the Crimson King*, issued October 10, 1969, which, given its hit status and fierce prog-rocking credentials, just might make it the first prog album proper. Also, early on there's Gentle Giant and Van der Graaf Generator. And, if you've noticed, every single one of these bands is British.

Where does Pink Floyd fit in all this and for that matter, why are we trying to shove them in this box? First off, let's address the fact that there are other things going on in rock as Pink Floyd is issuing *The Dark Side of the Moon*. Big bands on the beat include Led Zeppelin, Black Sabbath, Deep Purple, and Uriah Heep, and it wasn't uncommon to consider Pink Floyd somewhat of a "hard rock" band. Let's also not forget, perhaps partly stemming from this, that Floyd is regularly cited as a favorite band of heavy metal fans and indeed, still garner votes in metal polls.

Also, a big deal at the time in the U.K. was glam rock, with the likes of Sweet, Slade, Mott the Hoople, and T. Rex doing well. Top of the heap was David Bowie. Marc Bolan was like a new Syd Barrett and Bowie's first three albums sound like Syd at work (and play).

But Syd Barrett wasn't in this new version of Pink Floyd and Syd-less or not, it's problematic calling them prog. The glaring divergence is that Pink Floyd are decidedly not about odd time signatures and manic virtuosic guitars and keyboards and bass and drums. Way at the red-hot end of the note-density scale is prog (and fusion, and jazz) and as you sashay down past heavy metal toward funk, glam, folk, pop, pub rock, and proto-punk, arguably, way at the sleepy end, there's Pink Floyd. Of course, it's deceptively

Caped and often wisecracking Yes keyboardist Rick Wakeman, 1976

so. Floyd's predilection for a cozy, gauzy, sonic recline is a belabored quiltwork of fussy layers, textures, and movements. Still, for the most part, the band is famous for sounding very laid-back, and that is the opposite of the raison d'être for prog.

So why is Pink Floyd considered a prog band at all? Well, that would have to do with other characteristics that are every bit as emblematic of prog, such as substantial song lengths as well as short bits or anything that doesn't adhere to the structure of a three-minute song with three verses and choruses and one break. Also, part of this is the presence of long instrumental passages. Then, as alluded to, there's the conceptual nature, manifesting in full concept albums. Pink Floyd did this more often than most prog bands. The band's Hipgnosis cover art also contributes to the sentiment, being arty, mysterious, and often elaborate and gatefolded.

More general and abstract, however, and most high concept, would be the band's

tendency to take the listener on a journey, either on record or live, creating a sense of seriousness through the creation of good music, crafted music, music for musos, even if, again, no one would ever accuse Rick or Nick or Dave of being flashy, of showing off.

All told, what I find most interesting about this exercise is the fact that Pink Floyd had quite a hand in setting all this up, and then had to stand by and watch while a good ten or twelve albums better than theirs came out during 1971 and 1972 using roughly the same musical language. *The Dark Side of the Moon* would change all that, putting Pink Floyd at the front. In fact, through the record's understated sophistication and maturity, Pink Floyd would, in effect, arrive at prog and then transcend it in one fell swoop, repeating a sort of vanquishing of the stagnating genre fully three more times before the decade was out, which represents, after all, the most salient meaning of the word "progressive."

"ECLIPSE (A PIECE FOR ASSORTED LUNATICS)"

It seems absurd, surreal, or at least improbable that Pink Floyd would play anything from such a formal and high-fidelity album as *Dark Side of the Moon* before the elaborate production thereof, but that's exactly what they did. And not just the odd work in progress, but all of it. And for a whole year before the album would come out and change the lives of its creators.

Typical of the band's fearlessness, the guys had decided at a meeting at Nick's house in Camden that playing unreleased music might be the way to go, next convening at Decca Studios in Hampstead on November 10 through December 10, 1971, to write and record demos of the material. They next transitioned to a Rolling Stones–owned warehouse to rehearse for the tour, performing the new compositions at three days of dress rehearsals, January 17–19 of the new year at the Rainbow Theatre in Finsbury Park. These sessions also served as a test run for the band's new quadraphonic sound system. This was followed by a first attempt at the whole record, on January 20, aborted due to technical issues with the prerecorded effects for "Money," and then the first successful playthrough the following night at the Portsmouth Guildhall.

The press got to see it ten shows later back at the Rainbow, where it was christened "The Dark Side of the Moon: A Piece for Assorted Lunatics," changed from working title "Eclipse." The program included the complete lyrics to the song suite. After U.K.

ECLIPSE
(A Piece For Assorted Lunatics)

By
PINK FLOYD

Medicine Head (above),
along with an ad for their
1972 album, *Dark Side of the
Moon* (left)

duo Medicine Head issued an album in '72 called *Dark Side of the Moon*, Floyd went back to "Eclipse," putting the subtitle in parentheses. As soon as the Medicine Head album sank without a trace, Pink Floyd reverted to "Dark Side of the Moon," used for the final North American leg in September and mainland European dates in November and December—Japan got this show as well, in March of '72.

The material didn't go through all that many changes from stage to vinyl, other than a huge uptick in performance and production. Even the "Speak to Me" intro effects emerged relatively intact. Most different is the existence of a (disciplined) six-minute jam called "Travel Sequence," which, the following year, became the much more polished and futuristic "On the Run." "Time" is slower, more ragged, sung an octave lower with pronounced harmonies. At the beginning

there was no "The Great Gig in the Sky;" in its stead sat "The Mortality Sequence" (also called "Religion"), 4 minutes of church-y organ washes overlaid with spoken-word effects, essentially samples of pastors reading Bible passages. By September, Rick had knocked the replacement piece into shape.

Over to side two of the show, as it were, the Booker T & the M.G.s–influenced "Money" rocked pretty hard, due to David's vigorous guitars, and the rest of the show stayed pretty faithful to what we'd eventually hear on the record, although "Any Colour You Like" early on went by the working title "Scat," due to David's wordless scat singing in the song. The "Eclipse" finale wasn't there at the very beginning, having been added February 10, 1972.

By the end of this remarkable run, the band essentially had *The Dark Side of the Moon* sorted, save for the pretty important

contributions of Dick Parry on sax and Clare Torry on vocals, and a real actualization of the audiophile effects. Played after the politely received new material (more than politely received, actually—press reports were effusive, with the hoopla resulting in a bootleg recording that sold over 100,000 copies), the band performed, variously, "One of These Days," "Careful with That Axe, Eugene," "Set the Controls for the Heart of the Sun," "Echoes," "A Saucerful of Secrets," "Blues," and "Childhood's End." The order of new to old would be flipped once the album emerged in the spring of 1973, with the band's bold and nifty idea paying dividends as *The Dark Side of the Moon* started selling in droves, now, ingeniously enough, as both a new studio album and reverse time-traveling talisman reminding the purchaser of the time they saw, somewhat perplexed, the record presented live in concert.

EMI   TG12345/D943A   EMI   TG12345/D943A   EMI
E.M.I. LTD.   E.M.I. LTD.
ENGLAND.   ENGLAND.

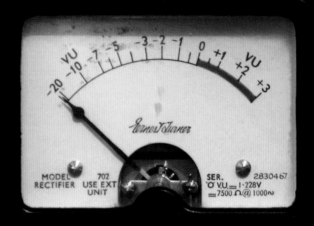
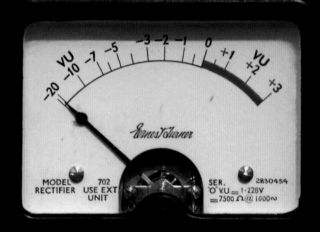

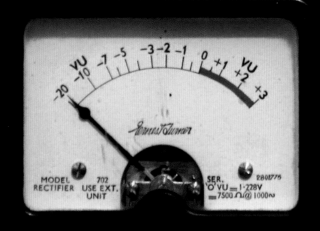
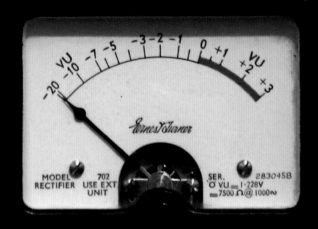

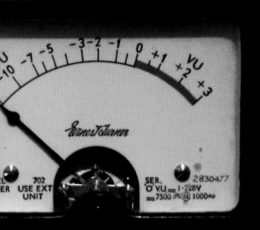

2 The Sessions

"You lock the door and throw away the key"

One might establish the first "session" toward the making of *The Dark Side of the Moon* as the band meeting at Nick's place, at which Roger's idea of a continuous conceptual piece about things that "make people mad" was first sketched out. This was followed by Roger hiding away in his garden shed studio out back of his Islington home and creating a few demos of the material that they had collectively begun writing. Next came working on the material through twelve days of rehearsals at Decca Studios in West London, followed by the live-show rehearsals at The Rolling Stones' 47 Bermondsey Street warehouse and then, innovatively, the touring of the "Eclipse" suite.

Inextricably linked with EMI, Abbey Road Studios, open for business November 12, 1931, had at times been state of the art and sometimes not. Pink Floyd had recorded there regularly over the years (although not exclusively), with the most significant recent visits being for *Atom Heart Mother* and portions of *Meddle*. Significantly, the band felt they had to move on from Abbey Road to finish "Echoes" (comprising all of side two of *Meddle*) because, at the time, it was limited to eight-track recording. Nearby, both AIR and Morgan had sixteen-track facilities, which Abbey Road acquired in time for *Dark Side*.

A detail of the Abbey Road Studios EMI TH12345 MK IV recording console, which Pink Floyd used to record *The Dark Side of the Moon*. The photo was taken before the console's auction through Bonhams in March 2017.

ABOVE: Abbey Road Studios in Maida Vale, North London, photographed January 25, 2022

OPPOSITE TOP & BOTTOM RIGHT: A wider-angle view of—and detail from—the recording console pictured in the chapter introduction

OPPOSITE BOTTOM LEFT: Alan Parsons at the mixing desk in the control room of Media Sound Studios in New York, 1979. As the engineer on *Dark Side*, Parsons is adamant the album was a sixteen-track affair.

For a mixing board, Abbey Road now had an EMI TG12345, its first solid-state, replacing the REDD .51, which was vacuum-tube based. The new console featured twenty-four microphone inputs and eight tape outputs, which came in handy, given the complexity of the sound effects the guys wanted on the album. Alan Parsons, engineer on the project, is emphatic, however, that the making of the record was essentially a sixteen-track production ("twenty-four channels into sixteen groups"), with many of the tracks being second generation because the band had run out of tracking room and had to consolidate and bounce first-generation tracks (the "Money" loop alone took up four tracks). The mix was conducted off the second-generation recordings, i.e., second-generation basic/backing tracks plus overdubs.

As Parsons told me, "Being an engineer for Pink Floyd was arguably the biggest challenge I ever gave myself. They're so sound oriented; they used the studio to the absolute maximum. So it was a big challenge as an

engineer. But I think I learned a bit and I think they learned from me as well (laughs). It was a really good team effort overall."

Asked about his Abbey Road employers George Martin and Geoff Emerick, Parsons says, "They were both mentors to me. I mean, Geoff Emerick is an amazing engineer, of course, and George, I consider that probably, to a certain extent, I modeled myself on him because he commanded enormous respect from every artist he worked with and he respected them, and so that's why he was the perfect inspiration."

Of course, Abbey Road had essentially served as headquarters for The Beatles. Floyd would return there for work on *Wish You Were Here* and portions of *The Final Cut* and *The Division Bell*. The two Syd Barrett albums were cobbled together there, and Roger as a solo artist would use the facility as well.

Work on *The Dark Side of the Moon* began at Studio 3 on June 1, 1972, after the band had returned from dates in West Germany and the Netherlands, the culmination of about forty shows playing the whole album live. Typically the band worked from 2:30 in the afternoon until midnight. The first song worked on was "Us and Them," with the band

OPPOSITE: A view of Abbey Road Studios, Studio 3 in July 2013. Work on the album began here on June 1, 1972.

ABOVE LEFT: Producer George Martin, pictured in London in the early '90s. Parsons has said he modeled himself after Martin to an extent because of the respect the producer received from artists.

ABOVE RIGHT: Pink Floyd perform as part of the Amsterdam Rock Circus at the Olympisch Stadion, Amsterdam, May 22, 1972

RIGHT: The Allison Research TR804 Kepex (Keyable Program Expander) is used for gating effect and noise control, i.e., "cleaning up" errant noise, often with respect to drums.

BELOW: The EMS Synthi AKS synthesizer allowed the band to create loops, most famously for "On the Run."

OPPOSITE: The band recorded sporadically over two weeks beginning January 18, 1973, in Studio 2 (seen here) before moving over to Studio 3.

sticking with Studio 3 for three days. Parsons had worked with The Beatles by this point but had also served as assistant tape operator on *Atom Heart Mother*, so he knew the guys well.

Work then shifted to Studio 2, June 6–10, where the basic tracks for "Money" were recorded on June 7 and "Time" the following day (Gilmour's use of a Kepex processor for tremolo can be heard on "Money"). Roger had originally captured the sound effects for "Money" by recording on a Revox A77 the sounds of coins and other items tossed into a mixing bowl in his wife's pottery studio and then splicing tape the old-fashioned way, working with the song's 7/8 time-signature. But this got rerecorded in the studio, given the possibility of improving it for the planned quadraphonic mix. One can hear a cash register (from a sound library record), an adding machine (Alan's contribution), and paper tearing. Nick recalls drilling holes in old pennies and threading them onto strings to help create the innovative sonic symphony.

After two days off, it was back to work again at the same locale, June 13–17, followed by a move back to Studio 3, June 20–25, where the basic tracks were recorded for "The Great Gig in the Sky" on the final day.

Besides the new mixing board, also crucial to the process was the cutting-edge EMS Synthi AKS synthesizer, which allowed the band to create loops, most famously for "On the Run," where Gilmour and Waters collaborated on the effect. This was also used for the solo on "Any Colour You Like."

As for the band's individual tools of the trade, Rick Wright made use of a Wurlitzer organ through a wah pedal and utilized other synth technologies, such as the ARP String Ensemble and the Minimoog. There's also a Fender

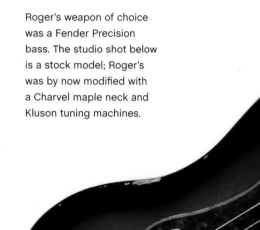

Roger's weapon of choice was a Fender Precision bass. The studio shot below is a stock model; Roger's was by now modified with a Charvel maple neck and Kluson tuning machines.

Rhodes on "Breathe" and classic Hammond sounds at the end of "Eclipse." "Brain Damage" features both Hammond and Minimoog.

Roger's weapon of choice was the Fender Precision bass he'd been using since 1970, modified at this point with a maple neck by Charvel and Kluson tuning machines. David used his black 1969 Fender Stratocaster, which he later modified many times, soon with an additional switch that allowed him to manipulate the pickups to evoke the sound of a Fender Jazzmaster, and then with a Gibson PAF humbucker in time for the shows

RIGHT & TOP: David's black Fender Stratocaster is handled with white gloves at Christie's in London—and handled by the maestro himself at Detroit's Olympia Stadium in June 1975.

ABOVE: David's Hiwatt amplifiers are on view in this shot from Olympia Stadium, Detroit, Michigan, June 24, 1975.

OPPOSITE: David's pedal steel can be heard on "Breathe" and "The Great Gig in the Sky."

ABOVE: A Moog Minimoog synthesizer, as utilized by Rick Wright

BELOW LEFT: The Italian-made Binson Echorec echo machine provided David's guitars with a delay effect superior to that offered by older machines that relied on magnetic tape.

BELOW RIGHT: David's Dallas Arbiter Fuzz Face effects pedal was one of the main tools in his arsenal.

with Roland Petit's Ballets de Marseille in early 1973. Also, notably on "Money" (and probably "Brain Damage," "Us and Them," and "Eclipse"), Gilmour played a 1970 mahogany-body custom Bill Lewis guitar with twenty-four frets. On "Money" this was used specifically to get the high notes in the third part of his solo. On "Breathe" and "Great Gig in the Sky" you can hear a Fender 1000 twin-neck pedal steel.

For effects, Gilmour used a Dallas Arbiter Fuzz Face (BC108), a Colorsound Powerboost, a Univox Uni-Vibe, Binson Echorec II and PE 603, the aforementioned Kepex processor, and the EMS Synthi Hi-Fli guitar effect processor, which was a prototype version Gilmour bought from the manufacturer in 1972 at great expense. But effects were minimal, given there was nothing digital out at the time. Parsons indicates that most of his sounds were coming right out of the cabinets, augmented perhaps with a plate reverb or tape delay.

In the amp department, Gilmour used Hiwatt DR103 All Purpose 100-watt heads, a Fender Twin Reverb silverface 100-watt combo, a Maestro Rover rotating speaker, a Leslie rotating speaker cabinet (plus effects simulating Leslies), and WEM Super Starfinder 200 cabinets, which Parsons mic'd with Neumann U87s or U86s placed a foot in front of the cabinets. The classic Leslie rotating speaker effect can be heard on "Breathe."

Nick Mason was partial to his seven-piece Ludwig Silver Sparkle kit but notably played Rototoms, tuned to the chord changes, on the intro to "Time." For cymbals, he consistently used an array of Paistes. Mason originally played Premiere as he was endorsed by them but had moved over to Ludwig by 1970 (at first without endorsement) and stayed until 1992. (He also played Gretsch for a brief period.) Mason gets a solo credit on "Speak to Me," given that it was something that he had first worked up at home, proving his ability to be tech-minded as well. Also on the drum front, the pervasive heartbeat throughout the album is a gated bass drum (with lots of EQ at 100 Hz), using the Kepex noise gate technology that was new at the time.

Although Parsons had mic'd Mason's kit elaborately, he used only four tracks for drums. One of the more enigmatic bits from Nick is the repeating single-stroke roll high-hat that drives "On the Run," given the

Nick takes a break from recording the drums for the Children in Need charity version of "All You Need Is Love" in 2009 at Abbey Road.

The cast of *Monty Python's Flying Circus*, plus the Arsenal football crest—both *Python* and Arsenal were welcome distractions for the band from the pressures of music making.

dovetailing of a short and shocking "hit" of distortion that sort of torments his high-hat part. But as Parson explains, what sounds like a lot of complication on "On the Run" is mostly a one-man show conducted by Dave, utilizing what was essentially a mono feed from a single synthesizer.

Concerning the legendary cacophony of alarm clocks on "Time," that was something that Parsons had previously put together for a quadraphonic test record for EMI, recording each clock separately in an antiques shop in Hampstead. Quad was being touted at the time as the next evolution beyond stereo, and Parsons and Pink Floyd were ready participants—*Atom Heart Mother*, *Dark Side of the Moon*, and *Wish You Were Here* would all come out on quad. Parsons took a portable tape machine to the shop and had to have the proprietor stop all the clocks so Parsons could capture them one at a time. Also on the effects front, explained Alan, "The footsteps on the intro to 'On the Run,' that was me and my assistant engineer, Pete James, pacing the floor at #2 studio at Abbey Road."

After some time off (but also more shows), there were further *Dark Side* sessions on October 10–12 and 17, 1972, followed by a show at Wembley Empire Pool on the October 21. Work resumed October 25–27, but then the band was sent back on the road in mainland Europe in November. Work would often be interrupted to watch *Monty Python's Flying Circus*, or to allow Roger to cheer on his beloved Arsenal FC. Parsons has said that he'd stay behind and keep working during the breaks for *Monty Python*, recalling that this is when he'd get some of his best ideas down on tape.

Rehearsals in advance of the final recording sessions took place January 9, 1973, with the band recording sporadically over two weeks beginning January 18 in Studio 2 before moving over permanently to Studio 3. At this point the band recorded "Brain Damage," "Eclipse," "Any Colour You Like," and "On the Run," plus overdubs needed for the basic tracks from earlier sessions. Mason recalls that "Any Colour You Like" was a two-chord jam cooked up on the spot to fill space, with the highlight being Gilmour's guitar solo. Dick Parry's sax parts were recorded for "Money" and "Us and Them" (using a 1969 Henri Selmer tenor sax) plus four female backing vocalists—Doris Troy, Lesley Duncan, Liza Strike, and Barry St. John—were brought in to sing on "Brain Damage," "Eclipse," and "Time." Their voices were fed through a pitch-shifter to achieve a sweeping effect. Of note, also on the vocal front, Parsons double-tracked most of the lead vocals, adding effects like reverb and delay.

Clare Torry's vocals for "The Great Gig in the Sky" were recorded on January 21 with the sessions wrapping up February 1. Noted Parsons, "I suggested calling up Clare Torry to sing 'Great Gig in the Sky'—they were unacquainted with her. There were a few specific instances like that where I injected some, you know, ideas."

Torry did three or four takes of the suggested wordless vocal, with Parsons indicating that the final performance was a composite. Torry remembers fondly the excellent mix Parsons got between her voice and the music in her headphones and greatly enjoyed closing her eyes and belting it out, once she had a firm grasp on the concept. Torry also recalls that the guys (other than Dave) looked completely bored during the process and she was ushered out quickly after she was done, feeling as she left that she probably was not going to make the record.

At the end of the process, producer Chris Thomas was brought in to check out the final mixes. He recalls picking up the task at midnight and then driving over to AIR to work until 5 a.m. on *Grand Hotel*, his third of what would be four records in a row for Procol Harum.

Although he doesn't admit to any disputes, apparently there was indeed vehement disagreement about the final mix, with Roger and Nick wanting a drier sound emphasizing the sound effects on the album and David and Rick wanting more echo, emphasizing the songs and melodies. In fact, Chris was called in as mediator; both David and Rick would hover over him at different times, willing the faders to move their way, to the point where both ended up in the control room with him (Gilmour says he got his way). Then there was Alan, who wasn't happy with Thomas's propensity to "limit" the drums. Parsons later regretted that the drum sound could have been better.

Notably, Thomas was also at the Clare Torry session on "The Great Gig in the Sky," and proved instrumental in synchronizing the echo on "Us and Them." Parsons recalled that Chris had rode him hard to locate the "magic" rough mixes for the Rototoms used at the beginning of "Time," but they were unsuccessful in their search. In the final analysis however, after three weeks of work, all parties were more than pleased with *The Dark Side of the Moon*. All that was left was to tour a record that actually existed.

QUESTIONS

Brian Eno co-created the Oblique Strategies card system to help jog the gods of creativity into coughing up unexpected congruencies. Roger Waters took a less formal route toward the same mysterious place of creation, whereby the sum of small parts blossomed into something larger. With a strategy of using snippets of dialog across the record—sometimes barely audible, sometimes the center of attention—Waters came up with a set of flashcards with questions written on them, beginning benign and working up to more invasive enquiries regarding views on violence, madness, and death.

A typical session featured some variant of the following: "What's your favorite color? Why do rock 'n' roll bands split up? When was the last time you thumped someone? Why did you do it? Did you think you were in the right? Do you still think you were in the right? Are you frightened of dying? Why are you frightened of dying? Do you ever think about the dark side of the moon? Do you ever think you're going mad? If so, why? What do you think of *The Dark Side of the Moon*?"

Roger got the idea from being lightly interrogated, along with the rest of the band, by director Adrian Maben, who had been asked to come by the studio and get some extra footage to add to *Live at Pompeii*. Maben asked the band innocuous questions but also touched upon the tension in the band now that they had been together five years. This inspired the question about bands breaking up.

And so, during the final week of recording, beginning January 22, 1973, Roger asked approximately twenty "willing guinea pigs," ranging from Apple studio staffers to Pink Floyd roadies and their girlfriends, to sit in a darkened Studio 3 and speak their responses into a microphone as questions were read from the cards stacked on a conductor's stand. Paul McCartney had been finishing up *Red Rose Speedway* next door, and he and Linda were game to give it a go, but Roger deemed their responses unusable because they were trying too hard and sort of performing. David remarked that they were "much too good at being evasive."

Roger's plan was to use the spoken words as bridge material between the songs, as well as elsewhere in the compositions. In the end, roadie Chris Adamson provided the words placed low in the mix behind the heartbeat that dominates opener "Speak to Me": "I've been mad for fucking years, absolutely years." Road manager Peter Watts is also in "Speak to Me," providing the uneasy laughter, which can also be heard in the pivotal "Brain Damage."

Another key contribution comes from Roger "the Hat" Manifold, who was a road manager for several bands. He's nicknamed as such because he'd wear a formal top hat while out in the street conducting his business. Manifold was recorded at the end of the process. Having misplaced the notecards, Roger asked him questions without the visual aids while David recorded the exchange back in the control room. He can be heard saying, "Live for today, gone tomorrow, ha ha ha" on "On the Run" and "short, sharp shock" on "Us and Them." This came from an explanation of a road rage incident he admitted he instigated.

Also making it onto the record was Wings guitarist Henry McCullough ("I don't know... I was really drunk at the time" at the end of "Money"). Also, in this segue piece, among a barrage of additional voices, is Peter Watts' second wife, Patricia "Puddle" Watts, who

remarks about the "geezer" that is "cruisin' for a bruisin.'" Patricia also provides the line, "I never said I was frightened of dying" about a minute from the end of "The Great Gig in the Sky," with studio doorman Gerry O'Driscoll expressing somewhat the same sentiment at the beginning.

Finally, at the close of the entire album, at the 1:37 mark of "Eclipse," we get what is perhaps the highlight of the spoken-word process, with O'Driscoll, mixed quietly behind that oppressive beating heart we heard back at the beginning, informing us in his thick Irish accent, "There is no dark side of the moon, really; matter of fact, it's all dark."

OPPOSITE: Paul and Linda McCartney, 1973

LEFT: A page from the Pink Floyd edition of *Rock 'n' Roll Comics* details Roger's writing process.

ABOVE: Henry McCullough from Wings, 1972

SUPPORTING CAST

Asquinty read of *The Dark Side of the Moon*'s credits reveals that the Pink Floyd guys relied on a few outside support services along the way, many just fulfilling roles necessary to the making of any record, but a few providing signature icing-on-the-cake elements that help make the record so special. We've mentioned elsewhere assistant engineer Peter James, who served as Alan Parsons' right-hand man and provided the footstep sound effects (James would return to assist on *Wish You Were Here*). We've also told the story of the four backup singers dutifully included in the official credits.

Outside of the design credits, that leaves Clare Torry, Dick Parry, Alan Parsons, and Chris Thomas. We've outlined their contributions elsewhere as well, but their importance to the album warrants brief biographical attention.

CLARE TORRY, who provides the wordless vocal performance on "The Great Gig in the Sky," was born November 29, 1947, in London. Before appearing on *Dark Side*, she had recorded a handful of singles. After her tracking of the *Dark Side* song, she soon was onstage singing her part with the band on November 4, 1973, at the Rainbow Theatre in London. She also sang the song with the band at Knebworth in 1990 (and with Roger Waters at some solo shows), and appearing on Waters' second album, *Radio K.A.O.S*, and his collaborative soundtrack album for the animated film *When the Wind Blows*.

Torry went on to become, essentially, a working vocalist, singing in TV commercials and recording sessions, while also touring as a backup singer, most notably for the Alan Parsons Project, and singing the lead vocal on "Don't Hold Back" from the band's gold-certified *Eve* album. The standard fee for what she did on "The Great Gig in the Sky" was £15 but Torry said she charged Pink Floyd double because it was a Sunday. In 2004, Torry successfully sued the band and EMI, claiming that her work on "The Great Gig in the Sky" constituted some measure of a songwriting credit. The parties settled for an undisclosed amount with all subsequent issues of the album specifying "Vocal composition by Clare Torry."

Saxophonist DICK PARRY, born December 22, 1942, in Suffolk, England, appears twice on *Dark Side*, but also on *Wish You Were Here*'s "Shine On You Crazy Diamond" and "Wearing the Inside Out" from Pink Floyd's 1994 album *The Division Bell*. Parry was brought into the fold as a friend of David Gilmour, indeed going on to play live with Gilmour the solo artist in 2001, 2002, and 2006. Parry was also brought on during the Pink Floyd reunion for Live 8 to replicate his historic solo from "Money." Other career highlights include touring as part of The Who's brass section in 1979 and 1980 and touring with the Violent Femmes in Europe and South Africa.

ALAN PARSONS, born December 20, 1948, in London, began his career at the age of eighteen in October 1967 as an assistant engineer at Abbey Road Studios. By the recording of *Dark Side*, he had already worked with the Floyd guys on *Atom Heart Mother*, but he'd also engineered on The Beatles' *Let It Be*, *Wild Life* from Wings, and *Stormcock* by Roy Harper, with *Dark Side* being a big step up in responsibility and complexity.

Parsons declined the offer to work on *Wish You Were Here*, instead starting the Alan Parsons Project with Scottish songwriter Eric Woolfson and issuing a debut album in 1976 called *Tales of Mystery and Imagination*. The band racked up multiple gold and platinum awards across ten studio albums between 1975 and 1987, selling an estimated 50 million copies worldwide. In between albums, Parsons didn't do much producing, with his most notable credit being *Year of the Cat* by Al Stewart. After his charmed run with the eponymous band, Parsons went on to become a solo artist, issuing five albums to date while taking on occasional studio work.

Storied producer CHRIS THOMAS served as a late collaborator on the final mix. Born January 13, 1947, in Middlesex, England, Thomas came up much like Parsons, having been thrown into the room, solo, with The Beatles to finish up *The Beatles*, also known as "The White Album." He came in as mix supervisor on *Dark Side* on the strength of his work assisting George Martin but also on his track record with Procol Harum (simultaneously, he'd begin a long association with Roxy Music). Thomas would go on to produce Badfinger and, most famously, *Never Mind the Bollocks, Here's the Sex Pistols*, in 1977. This was followed by an impressive number of credits with the likes of Pete Townshend, The Pretenders, The Human League, INXS, and, very regularly, Elton John. Thomas also worked with David Gilmour on his 2006 solo album *On an Island*.

OPPOSITE: Clare Torry in London, June 1969

ABOVE: Dick Parry, on tour with Pink Floyd in 1975

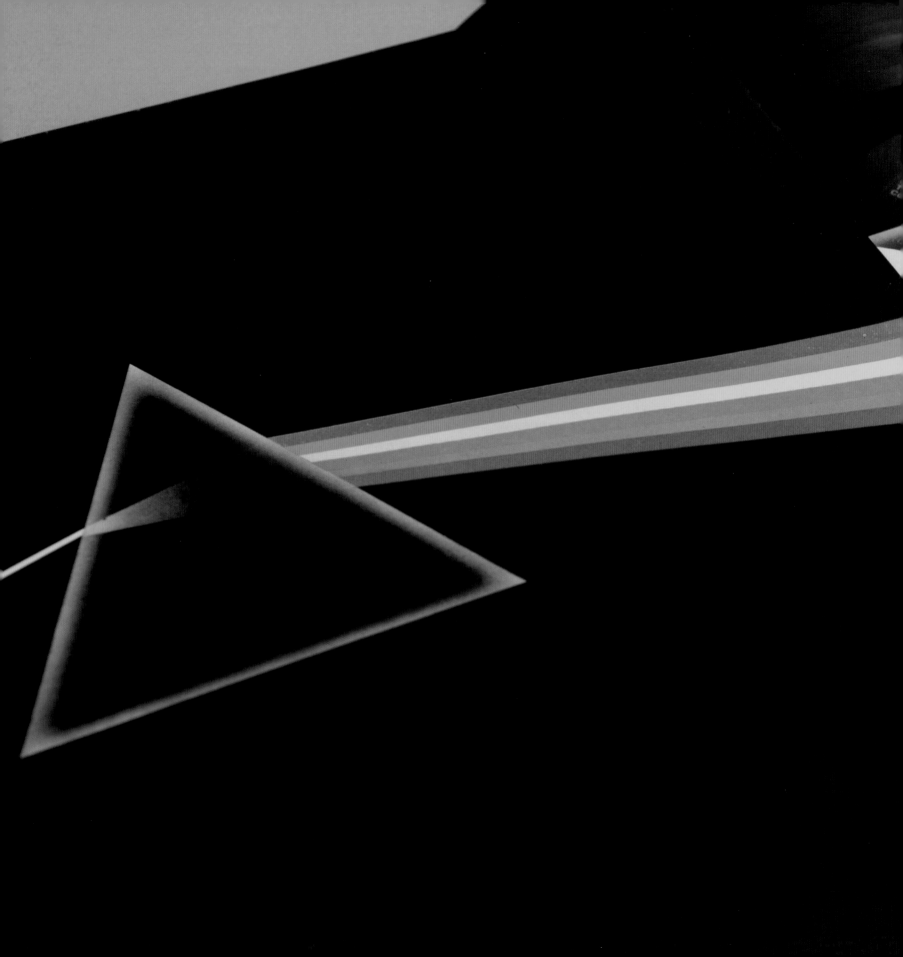

Arguably the
most iconic
album packaging
of the rock era

3 The Art and Packaging

"All that you touch and all that you see"

In much the same manner that the sound effects and
recorded bits of dialog captured for inclusion on the record
created a synergy, an effect where the sum is greater than
the parts, so too would the graphics created for *The Dark
Side of the Moon*, given that the elements chosen were in no
way particularly lunar or otherwise literal.

Storm Thorgerson from the Hipgnosis graphics collective
(at the top it was Storm and Aubrey "Po" Powell), guilty
parties for most of the Pink Floyd jackets thus far, had seen a
photograph in a physics textbook of a prism refracting light.
He suggested this to associate George Hardie and it was off
to the races. Rick Wright had suggested that it would be nice
to see something "simple, clinical, and precise," Storm also
recalling him saying "graphic" and "stylish." Also, because it
would be a welcome change of pace to put aside the
photographic representations that Hipgnosis had cooked up
for Floyd so far, Hardie came up with the illustrated version
of the optical phenomenon, even though photographs did a
pretty good job of capturing the effect (as it turns out, the
depicted angle of refraction is impossible, so a photograph
perhaps wouldn't do anyway). The added twist was that when
one usually saw this effect drawn in science texts, if there

ABOVE: Storm Thorgerson, graphic designer and video director, on the set of the film *Tune* at the Royal College of Art film studio, London, March 9, 1967. Thorgerson was studying at the college at the time.

OPPOSITE: Rick Wright shooting film on a Minolta cine camera offstage at Hakone Aphrodite, Japan, August 6, 1971. It was Rick who had suggested something "simple, clinical, and precise."

was any color at all, it was usually depicted on a white background. Judging a black background to look "cool," Hardie set about creating a white mock-up with indications for the printer to reverse to black.

As Aubrey Powell explained the relationship to me, "George Hardie worked for Hipgnosis as an illustrator and designer. Because Storm Thorgerson and myself, the two partners who owned Hipgnosis, couldn't draw. Couldn't draw for toffee. And so, when we had something that needed illustrating, whether it was graphics or whether it was lyrics or design, or *Dark Side of the Moon*, for example, we drew that up and sold it to the band, an idea, on a piece of paper. And then had to have it drawn out professionally by an illustrator, because we couldn't draw that. So, we had George Hardie, and 'Please, could you draw this?' We were like family, all together. Hipgnosis worked as an art studio, I'd say, similar to Andy Warhol's Factory—we were a bit like that. Storm and I came up with the ideas, but we worked with a lot of assistants and a lot of people around us who could do things better than we could, so we would call upon them to do things for us. And as I said, George Hardie was one of them."

For the prism effect, Hardie came up with a line drawing representation and then indicated percentages of cyan (C), magenta (M), yellow (Y), and black (K) required to create rainbow colors using the standard "CMYK" four-color printing process. In the real world, when white light passes through a prism (or moisture, in the case of a rainbow), a seventh color, indigo, is present in the effect, but this was left out because it was deemed too close to the violet, hence the six distinct, blocked-off colors. The prism itself was an airbrushed illustration. There would be no band name or album title on the front cover, which would mark the fourth time in a row that Floyd had stood their ground against EMI's simple request to help sell the product enclosed. There were to be no pictures of the band on the front or back either, which, combined with the lack of wordage, added to the mystery, as well as the anonymity.

The band was presented with seven ideas in a basement room at Abbey Road, with a front-runner being a depiction of the Marvel Comics Silver Surfer figure, surfing the cosmos, which was deemed unrealistic due to nobody thinking they could secure the rights to use the character. As Storm remembers, it took them about 3 seconds to pick the prism from among the concepts that the Hipgnosis team had toiled over for weeks. He recalls the guys glancing at everything, picking the prism by

LEFT: A Jack Kirby Silver Surfer sketch. A version of the Marvel Comics hero was an early front runner for the album sleeve.

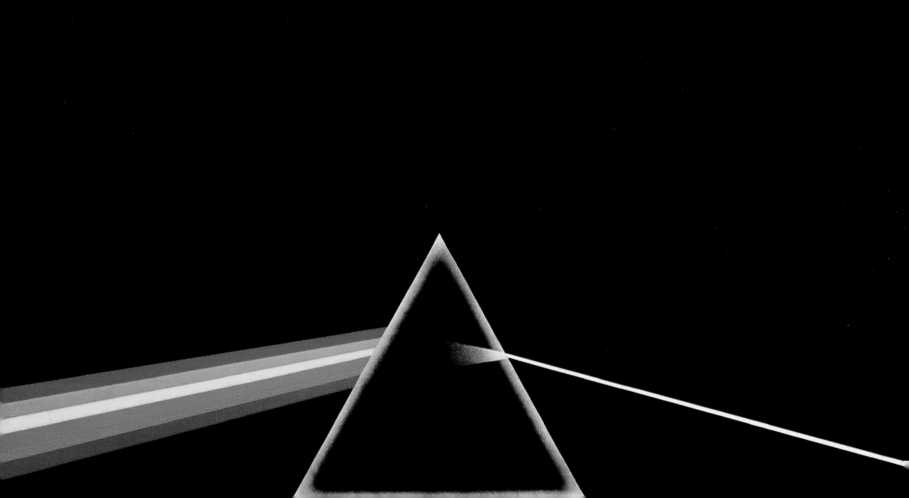

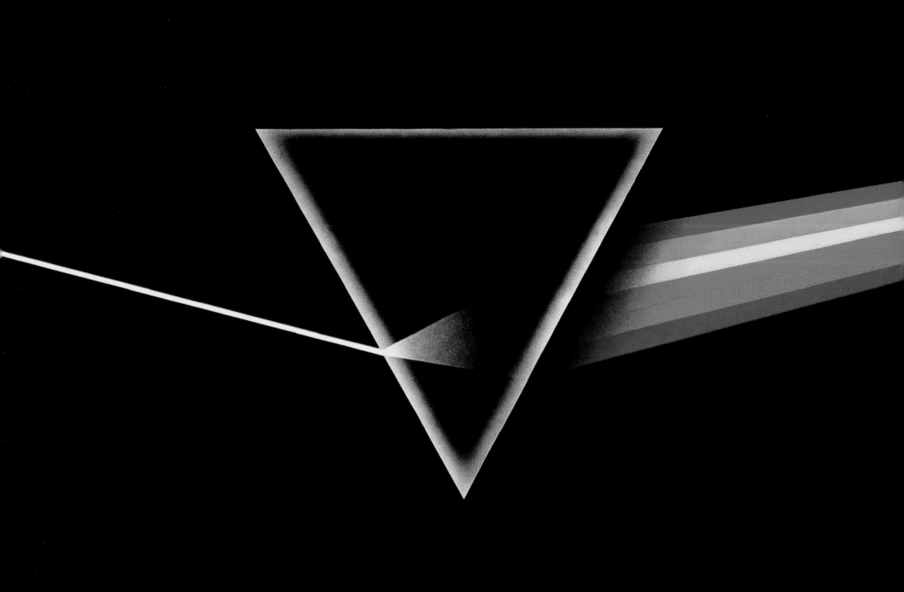

saying "That one," and then quickly heading back upstairs to work on the music to go on the record.

"Hipgnosis was rarely . . . how could I put it?" reflects Powell. "We rarely designed to something which was specifically about the topic to an album. And I quote Pink Floyd with this: they didn't go anywhere else. They just asked us to come up with the ideas and there was never any competition. And often [a] band came to us. I remember Hall and Oates came to us and said, 'Would you do a cover for us? . . . We're getting a bunch of designs.' And we'd say, 'Well, when you chuck those out the window, let us know, and then you can ask us to do it.' Because we didn't work with competition like that. We didn't want to waste our time. We had so much work going on. I think in that period of time, between '67 and '82, we did something like four hundred album covers. And we did a lot of other things too—advertising and lots of stuff, lots of different kinds of work . . . and we didn't have a digital world. You're doing it by hand, you took the photograph, you processed the film, you cut out the pictures, you stuck them together. It was a process that could take two months just to put one album cover together.

"To be honest with you," continues Aubrey, "Hipgnosis had a lot of power. We said, 'This is what you get—you get what you get.' We were very expensive. And we were considered by many bands, particularly the more well-known bands like Led Zeppelin or Pink Floyd or Peter Gabriel or Genesis or Yes or whatever it was, we were considered by them to be in a sense, part of the band. We didn't work for record companies, we only worked for bands. Or we rarely worked for record companies. Paid by the bands and worked directly with them and formed friendships with them. And we were considered to be very much very instrumental in creating images around their music and around the image that they wished to be portrayed.

"You have to go back and look at the '70s," says Powell. "There was no MTV, no VH1, no YouTube or stuff like that. There were very few rock 'n' roll TV shows in those days, and also very few magazines. We had *Rolling Stone*, *Melody Maker*, *New Musical Express*, and things like that, but there were not that many outlets to gain access to a band. And of course, the album cover became a representation of that. When people bought an album, it was a ritual. You've got the cover, you peeled off the shrink wrapping, looked inside for all the clues you wanted to know about your

PINK FLOYD   DARK SIDE OF THE MOON

band and the latest kind of information to get about them and it was very subtle. And there was the ritual of taking the record out, careful not to scratch it, putting it on the deck and then putting the needle down, playing the album.

"And at the same time, you're reading the lyrics or looking at the posters inside of the band or trying to work out what the cover was all about. So, there was an incredible ritual around our covers. And album covers often defined who you were. When you went to somebody's home, the albums that you had on the shelf . . . if you had 200 albums, you were a pretty cool guy. And if you looked at the covers that were there, if you had a load of Stones covers or Lynyrd Skynyrd, you knew what kind of person you were dealing with, as opposed to something like Mantovani or Burt Bacharach (laughs). So, they played a very intrinsic role."

But what does it all mean?

As it turns out, the triangle shape was chosen as a symbol of ambition, one of the album's themes, referring to the pressures of being an intense and busy band and the madness that might ensue, with the saga of Syd being one aspect of it. This is carried through elegantly and thoughtfully onto the six-panel 24 × 36-inch poster of pyramids tucked into the sleeve of the original vinyl presentation.

For this shot, because Hipgnosis takes their own pictures, Storm and Po flew to Giza, Egypt. There, Po fell ill, and it was left to Storm to traipse out in the night alone and take the photo of three pyramids at 2 a.m. using an infrared camera. He recalls the experience as "spooky," partly because to get the shot, he had crossed into an Egyptian army shooting range which resulted in a dressing-down from three angry soldiers who demanded payment. With "buckshee" having been paid, Thorgerson made sure to get a suggestion of moon, far off in the horizon, into the shot. Besides symbolizing ambition (or as Storm framed it "vaulted ambition") and madness, the pyramids also had something of the cosmic and mysterious to them, not to mention their association with death, a significant theme of the album. As well, there was the tacit suggestion, added to by the shot's nocturnal vibe, that *this* is what one will find on the dark side of the moon.

"You know, Hipgnosis reinvented itself weekly," chuckles Powell. "We just thought out of the box all the time. What is it that people are not expecting? What can we do? What do we like? We worked for us. We were

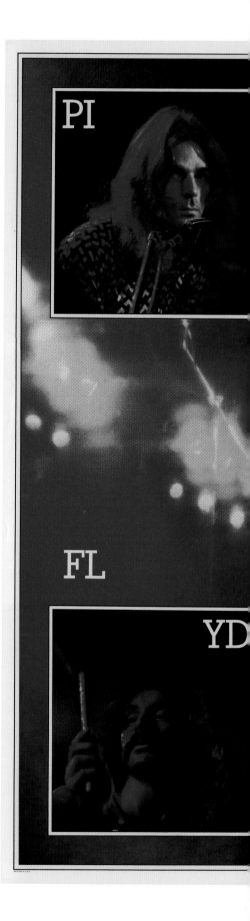

terribly selfish. Storm and I would think, what do *we* want to do? Where do you wanna go? I'd like to go to Hawaii. . .. And that used to happen every week (laughs). Every week, we'd going to Morocco or all over the world, doing different pictures. And we shot a lot in America, of course, because you have some wonderful landscapes there. In those days, people were like, 'Yeah, go, do it.' It's all part of the excitement you would generate in that '70s period. I mean, the halcyon days of album covers, between 1967 and 1982, which were the fifteen years that Hipgnosis operated, those fifteen years of album covers are an important cultural historical part of rock 'n' roll. And we celebrated like it was no tomorrow. We were doing whatever we wanted, wherever we wanted."

A second poster included with the album depicts the band live, with five inset shots floated over a typically shadowy, obscured image. This presentation echoes another theme redolent in the cover image, namely the importance of the band's live show. On the poster, the faces of the band members are blurred, in shadow, fighting with microphones and guitar necks. Nick, Rick, and David are shown once and Roger twice for a total of five squares. One of the Roger pictures and the shot of David are reversed, suggesting in error that they play left-handed. The full-band shot behind the boxes is backward too.

The arty text treatment on the poster, with the band name broken up into one or two letters per box, is carried over onto the two stickers also included with the package. The illustration is the same on both stickers, but the color scheme differs, with one representing day and one representing night, both with the same orange ball in the sky, one sun and one moon, which Roger framed as the epic duality of life force versus death force. The angular line drawing depicts the pyramids seen on the poster, along with palm trees. This is quintessential Hipgnosis illustration as applied to dozens of album covers for other bands.

Back to the exterior, the white light beam on the front is a continuation of a beam emanating from the back cover and across the spine. The rainbow effect on the right side of the cover lines up with the same on the left edge of the back cover, where the prism is inverted. Inside the gatefold, the prism effect also aligns left and right with both those on the front and back. This allowed for creative store displays using either the outside of the cover or the gatefold or both. Additionally on the gatefold, the ribbon of green from the middle of the rainbow is rendered as a sort

SMAS-11163-2

SMAS-11163-1

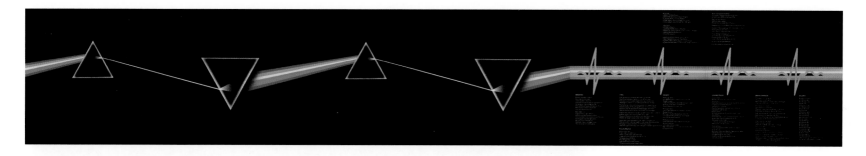

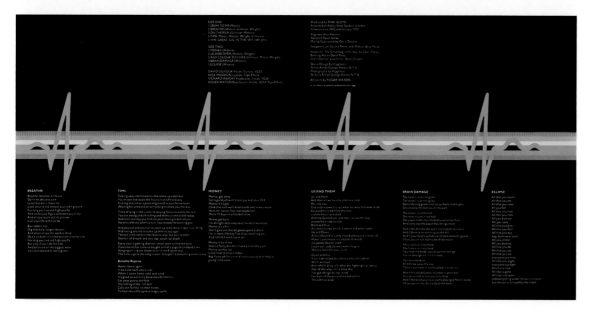

of EKG readout, representing the fact that a heartbeat begins and ends the album (this was Roger's idea). Credits above the line and lyrics below the line finish the inner gate. Again, because none of the bits and pieces were actual pictures of the moon, the outcome added substantial dimension beyond the lyrics and the music on the record.

"I would agree with the words you just used: edgy, sterile, precise," answers Aubrey, when I asked him about the Hipgnosis style. "Of course, there's no Photoshop, no digital way of working in those days, so it would have had to be done for real. We always did it for real. One of the key secrets to Hipgnosis was, if you look at our photographs carefully, everything was sharp focus front to back, which is not how the eye sees it—it's impossible. ... And what we did was create collages where everything in the foreground is crystal sharp. Let's take Styx as an

OPPOSITE: The stickers included with the package. Roger framed the night and day treatments as representative of the epic duality of life force versus death force.

ABOVE: The front, back, and inner gatefold of the sleeve line up to form a continuous image. But you'll have to purchase three copies to get the effect.

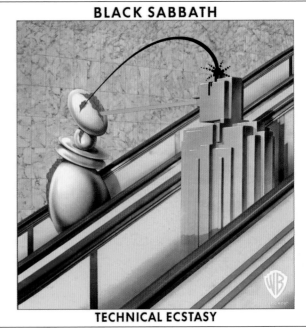

BLACK SABBATH

TECHNICAL ECSTASY

Two iconic Hipgnosis designs, showcasing illustration for Black Sabbath and the design house's characteristic photo-collaging for Styx's album *Pieces of Eight*.

example, *Pieces of Eight*. That's all a collage all put together, and if you look at it, everything is crystal sharp, from the earring in the foreground to the Easter Island figures in the back. And that's not how the eye sees things. It's a deliberate sort of approach, I suppose, almost pop art, in a way, how pop art sees things. You can paint like that, you can do cartoons like that, and we followed that way of doing things.

"If you look at Black Sabbath *Technical Ecstasy*, it's all sharp as an illustration. That was one of the things we looked for: edginess. I wanted to create things that were eye-catching, that were unusual, where people had to think about the cover and not just accept what was there. 'Oh, that's a pretty picture.' Think about what it meant, what had gone into it, what interpretation you wanted to put on it."

The effect of such good graphics, not to mention the enormous sales of the record, resulted in the prism image becoming the most enduring graphic representation associated with Pink Floyd. Rick Wright was proven correct in his aim to find something clean and classy and simple to associate with the band. The *Dark Side of the Moon* cover indeed fulfills this mandate, which, as they say, "looks good on a T-shirt"—a common quip in the industry with respect to what makes a good album cover. As

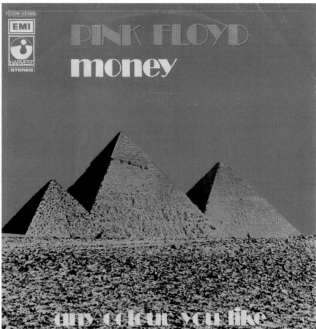

More pyramid power from Hipgnosis as applied to these two rare picture sleeves from Portugal (left) and Italy (right)

Gilmour has noted, the cover is both stark and commercial, telling *Rolling Stone* in 2003, "It wasn't a vague picture of four lads bouncing in the countryside. That fact wasn't lost on us."

More toward the abstract end, there's a palpable congruence between the cover art and the music from a production point of view. *The Dark Side of the Moon* is a precisely recorded album of standard-setting high fidelity for 1973, and the angular and scientific image on the front echoes the craftsmanship in the grooves enclosed—one could barely imagine a sleeve more diametrically opposed to both *Meddle* and *Obscured by Clouds*.

What's more, the two posters included with the package went up on bedroom walls around the world by the millions, serving as constant reminders that the pimply teenager contemplating life from behind the bedroom door and between the headphones should perhaps play *Dark Side of the Moon* right now and repeatedly if it is answers he or she seeks. Posters, stickers, apparel-ready iconography—what Hipgnosis did for *Dark Side* helped, materially, spread the word about the record they were wrapping.

WHO IS HIPGNOSIS?

Brought into being by Storm Thorgerson and Aubrey "Po" Powell in 1967, Hipgnosis went on to become the most famed record-cover design house ever, linked most closely with Pink Floyd. Storm had been in high school in Cambridge, with Syd a year behind him and Roger a year ahead, and had also been chums with David, who went to a different school. Roger and Storm played rugby and cricket together, plus their moms were pals. Aubrey, on the other hand, once leaving a different high school in Cambridge, took a number of knockabout jobs, but soon ended up as a set designer in television. Storm, Aubrey's roommate, was somewhat in the same business, having graduated with a Bachelor of Arts with an emphasis on philosophy and English but now studying for his MA in film and television at the Royal College of Art.

The company name was inspired by graffiti on the door to the guys' apartment. Being hip was cool, but so was the idea of the Gnostic, or esoteric mystical knowledge, as was the more obvious reference to hypnosis, which implied visuals so stunning that they might lock up and lock in the mind.

In 1968 Pink Floyd approached acquaintance David Henderson to paint the cover for their second album *A Saucerful of Secrets*, but he declined. Storm overheard the conversation and said he'd do it, having just tried his hand at some covers for some cowboy story paperbacks. It became the team's first commission with more to follow, first through EMI, Floyd's label. The early Hipgnosis designs were photographic, utilizing various tricks, as Storm and Aubrey took advantage of access to the Royal College of Art's darkroom facilities. Soon they'd have their own darkroom, in Aubrey's bathroom, and then in their own office at 6 Denmark Street.

Besides Floyd in '68 and '69, Hipgnosis did covers for the likes of Aynsley Dunbar Retaliation, Alexis Korner, pre-Uriah Heep band the Gods (twice), and Humble Pie. The quality and quantity of work exploded in 1970, with the designs for the self-titled from Quatermass, *Parachute* from Pretty Things, *Five Bridges* from The Nice, a second Aynsley Dunbar Retaliation sleeve, *Ring of Hands* from Argent, *King Progress* from Jackson Heights, and *Think Pink* from Twink. More notorious were the self-titled LPs from Cochise, featuring exposed breasts, and Toe Fat, which offered for our amusement two naked men with toes for heads.

The Hipgnosis style evolved through the early '70s with more complex photo trickery along with photo tinting, illustration, and elaborate custom lettering. Storm and Aubrey were constantly busy, famously charging customers no set fee but what they thought the final product was worth, which as Storm put it, only occasionally backfired.

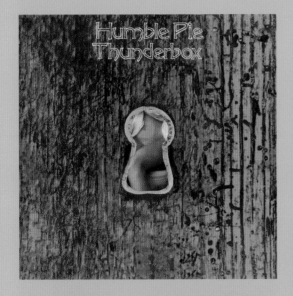

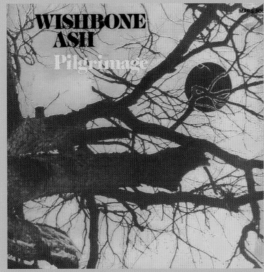

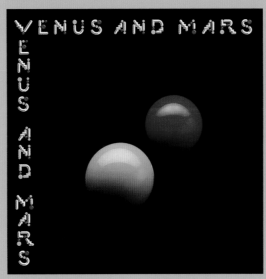

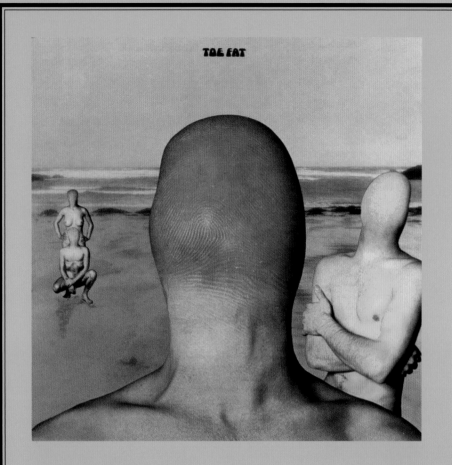

TOE FAT

GENESIS
THE LAMB LIES DOWN ON BROADWAY

GENESIS THE GODS

FIVE BRIDGES   THE NICE

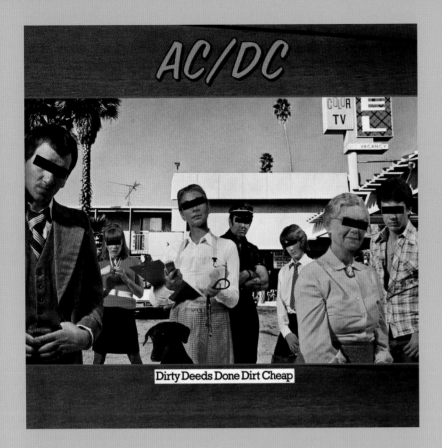

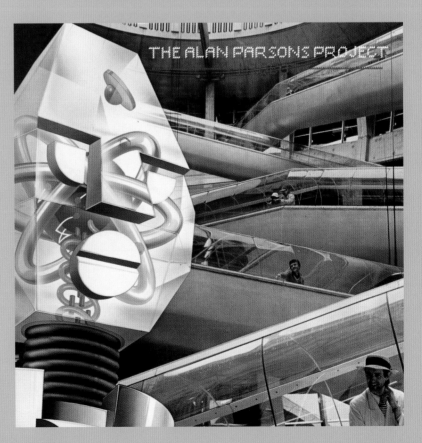

As the decade churned on (with Peter Christopherson joining in '74 and later becoming full partner), Hipgnosis did many landmark covers outside of the auspices of the Floyd. Just a few of the many highlights include Wishbone Ash's *Argus* and *Pilgrimage*; Led Zeppelin's *Houses of the Holy* and *Presence*; AC/DC's *Dirty Deeds Done Dirt Cheap*; Genesis's *The Lamb Lies Down on Broadway*; UFO's *Force It*, *Lights Out*, and *Obsession*; Golden Earring's *To the Hilt*; Black Sabbath's *Technical Ecstasy* and *Never Say Die!*; Alan Parsons Project's *I Robot* and *Eve*; and Rainbow's *Difficult to Cure*, plus many more, including multiple works for Wings, Al Stewart, Roy Harper, Brand X, Bad Company, 10cc, Electric Light Orchestra, and Peter Gabriel.

The firm broke up in 1983, with Aubrey moving into film production and Storm also working in video but continuing to add more high-profile covers to his resumé, before passing away from cancer, April 18, 2013, at the age of sixty-nine. "A constant force in my life," wrote Gilmour upon Storm's passing, "both at work and in private, a shoulder to cry on, and a great friend."

HIPGNOSIS AND PINK FLOYD
BEYOND THE DARK SIDE OF THE MOON

from a page of a 1967 *Doctor Strange* comic book, most prominently a portion that depicted a series of planets.

Next came the band's soundtrack album for the film *More*. For this one, Storm took a still from the movie that had figures cavorting around a windmill, flipped it to the negative, and then applied a nightmarish saturated orange and blue tint. Next, *Ummagumma* presents the band in a photo collage with Droste effect, essentially a picture within a picture within a picture ad infinitum, only—surprise—in the successive shots, the guys have switched positions.

For *Atom Heart Mother*, the band wanted to push back at psychedelic tropes, requesting something plain, a palette-cleanser symbolizing the band's desire not to be pinned to any genre. Storm drove out to the countryside and took a picture of the first cow he saw, and the

cover was cooked. There'd be no text included on the front, something Hipgnosis did most regularly with Pink Floyd but also for Led Zeppelin, notably for *Houses of the Holy* and *In Through the Out Door*.

With *Meddle*, however, the band was back at *Saucerful* and *More* terrain. Thorgerson's least favorite of the jobs he did for Floyd, the picture depicts a treated shot of an ear underwater taking in literal waves and sonic waves, which is sort of what we get with "Echoes" and even more so, "One of These Days." The gatefold makes up for all those times we didn't see who's in the band, with a stark, in-your-face, black-and-white shot of the guys sitting down, staring straight at the camera. Moving on, very much like *Meddle* is the sleeve for *Obscured by Clouds*, which featured a very out-of-focus picture of a man sitting in a tree.

Hipgnosis' austere job on *The Dark Side of the Moon* might be the most iconic album cover the firm created for Pink Floyd, but the relationship goes far beyond.

As discussed, the first cover was *A Saucerful of Secrets*, which essentially kicked off the company. The commission marked only the second time, first being for The Beatles, that EMI allowed a band to work with anybody but their own art department. The image used was an artful psychedelic shot that incorporated elements

With *Dark Side of the Moon* setting a new standard for both the band and their graphics house, Hipgnosis responded with the artwork for *A Nice Pair*, a repackaging of the band's first two albums. Nine squares featuring some unused Hipgnosis cover designs depicting mischievous visual puns (Hipgnosis often tried to get bands to buy into designs already rejected by the last lot of long-hairs through the door), along with some pictures committing visual puns directly on the title of the Floyd album at hand.

Wish You Were Here proved to be a second masterpiece of graphic trickery for the hippest design house in London. With Storm slaking deeply of the lyrics, he decided that the album was about absence. Ergo, the cover was wrapped in black cellophane, concealing the front cover art, on which two men shake hands, one of them on fire. On the back, there's a depiction of the concept of an "empty suit," and on the inner sleeve an orange wrap floats mysteriously in a field—

apparently there's a nude woman there. On a postcard (an instrument of absence), we see a woman diving into Mono Lake in California, somehow not causing any waves. In total, these shots were intended to represent earth, air, fire, and water. A sticker depicted two robot hands shaking, with the very Hipgnosis-like image by George Hardie also used for the labels applied to the vinyl.

Pink Floyd's *Animals* album from 1977, however, came wrapped in the best album cover story. For this one, Hipgnosis floated a giant inflatable pig over Battersea Power Station. The best pictures, with the most dramatic sky, were taken on the first day of shooting, although they couldn't get the pig to fly. On the second day, the pig became untethered and blew away in the wind, floating over Heathrow and causing canceled flights before landing in a farmer's field and scaring his cows. Storm and Aubrey had no choice but to airbrush the pig into the photos from the first day.

OPPOSITE TOP: Marvel cover for *Doctor Strange* #1, June 1968. Hipgnosis's cover for *A Saucerful of Secrets* was an artful psychedelic shot incorporating elements from another *Doctor Strange* comic.

OPPOSITE BOTTOM: As Deep Purple might say, "Who do we think we are?" The usually quite anonymous boys in Floyd answer that question boldly and plainly by way of the *Meddle* gatefold spread.

ABOVE: Pink Floyd celebrate the launch of the 2011 reissue campaign *Why Pink Floyd?* with a re-creation of the 1977 *Animals* cover at Battersea Power Station.

Hipgnosis didn't work on *The Wall* or *The Final Cut*. Roger had fired the firm for including the *Animals* cover in the first Hipgnosis book, *The Work of Hipgnosis: Walk Away René*, and not acknowledging him adequately enough for the original concept.

After the breaking up of Hipgnosis in 1983, with Roger gone from the band, the guys reunited with Storm Thorgerson for *A Momentary Lapse of Reason*. A story to rival that of the pig saga ensued, when 700 heavy wrought-iron beds were placed on a beach in Devon, only to have the rainy weather ruin the shot, causing the crew to have to repeat the exercise all over again two weeks later. For 1994's *The Division Bell*, Storm had two huge steel statues (designed by Keith Breeden and built by John Robertson) placed in a field. The two mechanical-looking busts were shown in profile, staring at each other, and could be seen as one head-on face as well, with the space between the two representing a *Wish You Were Here*–like absence, specifically that of Syd Barrett.

By this point, Thorgerson on his own had exhibited more of a signature style than he did back when it was him and Aubrey, utilizing time and again these expensive-looking surrealist photographic images. Beyond the two Pink Floyd studio albums, his eye for a well-crafted photograph with narrative would also be applied to the *Delicate Sound of Thunder* live album, the *Echoes* compilation, and the *Shine On* box set. In what serves as a final tribute to Gilmour's long relationship with Thorgerson, with Storm's passing in 2013, he reunited with Aubrey Powell to come up with the gorgeous— and very Storm-worthy—image used on Pink Floyd's final album, *The Endless River*.

For *A Momentary Lapse of Reason*, Hipgnosis placed 700 wrought-iron beds on a beach in Devon.

Side One

"Everything under the sun is in tune"

Speak to Me

Breathe (In the Air)

On the Run

Time

The Great Gig in the Sky

Travel back to March 1, 1973, with me if you will, and picture the first customers arriving home with their copy of *The Dark Side of the Moon*. Past the pleasant surprise of the stickers and posters sits the record. It's unsleeved and placed on the turntable. The needle is gently lowered.

Photo session in
Tokyo, March 1972

Speak to Me

What first confronts the listener is the pop of impregnation followed by silence, to be followed by more silence and then a heartbeat rising in volume, one second at a clip. This is "Speak to Me," 1:06 long unofficially because it wasn't made official on the original vinyl—there are no timings on the original U.K. pressing, or the American issue for that matter, where more often than not there are.

Credited to Nick Mason alone, the sound collage unsettles the listener, straining to hear what the haunting distant voices are saying, wondering why he hears clocks and cash registers, all while frantically trying to reset the hi-fi's volume levels against that woofer-provoking telltale heart. In the last 10 seconds the cacophony increases and there is nervous laughter and a mechanical helicopter effect. Also included is something that sounds like a single note played on an organ fading in and onto the scene (it is in fact a piano chord played by Rick Wright and then reversed on tape). He doesn't know it yet (although he might if he's read the lyrics on the bus home), but the emotions evoked in the listener are those that will be explored throughout the rest of the *Dark Side of the Moon*, namely anxiety, pressure, ambition, the passage of time, and the inevitable endpoint: death.

OPPOSITE: Nick Mason performs with the band at the Shelter National Campaign for the Homeless benefit concert at Earls Court Exhibition Hall in London, May 18, 1973.

What the listener also doesn't know is that these sounds will show up again on this journey, first the helicopter blades in "On the Run," then that nagging clock come "Time." Next and still on the first side of the original vinyl, the same woman's scream will be heard on "The Great Gig in the Sky." The robotic cash register effect will open side two's "Money" while crazy laughter will haunt another track called "Brain Damage." Finally, the heartbeat that hypnotized at the outset will also close the album, bookending it, fading at the end of "Eclipse." The sum of all this, the "becoming" heartbeat, followed by a cacophony, a rushing about, and ending in a woman screaming in pain tells us that someone is being born. And then what happens at the end of the record, at "Eclipse," is the opposite. A clue to this reading is embedded in the title. Essentially what the doctor is saying when he slaps the baby's bottom is "Tell me you're alive, tell me your heart is beating, speak to me."

As for that Nick Mason credit, there's a bit of mystery around it, with Nick claiming that the lion's share of the idea and the mechanical assembly of the sound picture came from him, but also the assertion from both Wright and Roger Waters that the credit might be a bit generous, made to provide Mason, usually not in on many credits, a bit of extra publishing monies. After Roger's bitter split with the band, he'd be known to complain about the whole thing, given how the album would become one of the bestselling records of all time.

Rick Wright at the Music Hall in Boston, Massachusetts, May 4, 1972

Breathe (In the Air)

"Speak to Me" shoots like a comet into "Breathe (In the Air)," credited at the music end to Wright and David Gilmour, with lyrics by Roger, who pens the entire album's worth of words. The song is sung by David, but it is his languid guitar work, making use of pedal steel, and a Uni-Vibe phase-shifter effect that sets about creating a legacy for Gilmour as the gold standard of a certain type of (barely) playing. Conversely, there's a busy enough bass line from Roger, Rick plays a sometimes surging but often polite Hammond organ and terminally smooth Fender Rhodes piano, while Nick provides a backbeat made airy by a ride cymbal. The song is only 2:49 long and there are no vocals until the halfway point, by which time David has gone a long way toward also establishing a signature singing style he'd make famous across the following three albums to close out the '70s.

As well, David's singing on the song, multitracked, matched his two guitar parts in delicate temperament. In fact, one might say the use of his voice against Roger's represents a female temperament, for the lyric finds a woman addressing her baby with philosophical musings upon

ABOVE: David used his UniVibe modulation effect on almost the entire *Eclipse* suite. When *Dark Side* came out in 1973, he was using it on just a few songs, notably "Breathe."

OPPOSITE: David plays his Fender Stratocaster through an expression pedal—perhaps the pedal used to control the speed of his UniVibe's effects—at the Shelter benefit in Earls Court.

what his life is about to entail—good, bad, indifferent, but fleeting and ultimately meaningless. The child is asked to go out in the world (but not forget Mother) and feel emotions and express identity. He's informed that living boldly is important, but in the end, the motions made and the breaths taken, the interactions, the touches, are what comprise life. This is all gently and hypnotically conveyed (and also sullied through a sigh of resignation), with the words delivered through a vocal performance that is the personification of drift and ennui. In fact, Roger has expressed that he knew David's voice suited the song better than his and acquiesced willingly.

The lyrical presentation consists of four verses, two each upon different chord sequences and no change in rhythm. Verses two and four both begin with the same line, while verses one and three begin with the same rhythmic cadence of words. It's a novel construct, with verses two and four sounding very much like a pre-chorus gesture, which then is not followed by a chorus.

As the song winds down—the entire time, it feels like it's unwinding—Roger's words shift to the theme of ambition, with the image of a running rabbit and holes being dug repeatedly. Then comes a softening of helpful advice, followed by the dagger. In mother's best-case scenario, baby-now-grown is juggling a busy life, riding the wave. He's then informed that it will all be for naught, a race to an early grave. We're left with more questions than answers, thrown into confusion by a mother's world-weary advice delivered from deep within a sort of subconscious state caused by an intravenous drip of a song.

At the risk of reading too much into the lyric—Roger later expressed a twinge of embarrassment at it, at least the opening couple of lines—the curious exhortation to "forget the sun" and the later mention of the tides brings us back to the idea of sun as life force and the moon as controlling death force, in this case driving the protagonist to an early grave whilst living up to its name, Luna, as in the lunacy of living to work, one of Roger's strong recurrent themes in songs and in interviews.

Pink Floyd in the
Netherlands, 1975

On the Run

Next up is "On the Run," which simultaneously illustrates the closing sentiments of "Breathe"—how jumping on the hamster wheel will lead to the heart giving out before its time—and also the more immediate theme that is the genesis of the story: how a band called Pink Floyd is burning itself out.

Indeed, in the early days, when the song was executed live between keyboards and guitars essentially, the idea was that "On the Run" was about the band's constant flying everywhere. The use of a prop airplane that crashes side-stage said as much, where the shift to more universal themes is represented by a flying bed, albeit years later, up into late 1987. The tacit message is that *Dark Side*, after years of its growing legend, is no longer about the band but about all of us (even if the flying bed also served the purpose of reminding people to go out and buy *A Momentary Lapse of Reason*).

But on the record, the narrative is one of a bustling airport, announcements threatening that the plane is boarding, the clock ticking, a man running to catch his flight. The innovative synthesizer and spoken-word collage—then Floyd's best and most extreme example to date using a device, almost a shtick, that would serve them well moving forward, especially on *The Wall*—sounds like airplanes and helicopters coming and going, maybe even the fuel trucks and baggage carts buzzing across the tarmac. It all ends in a harrowing plane crash that might mark the demise of a globetrotting rock band, but also a metaphor for the heart attack that might denote the end-stop in the more universal reading.

Ultimately "On the Run," despite essentially having no lyrics and being quite lengthy and not particularly action packed, save the ending, serves as a metaphor for the album itself, a compressed instrumental soundtrack piece to a movie called *The Dark Side of the Moon*. It also plays up one of the key devices that helped catapult Pink Floyd to fame: sound effects. In that sense it serves as a metaphor for the band as a whole and the career it built, in part, by giving us haunting voices.

Rick Wright at his Wurlitzer at the second of a three-night run at the Hippodrome in Birmingham, England, December 4, 1974

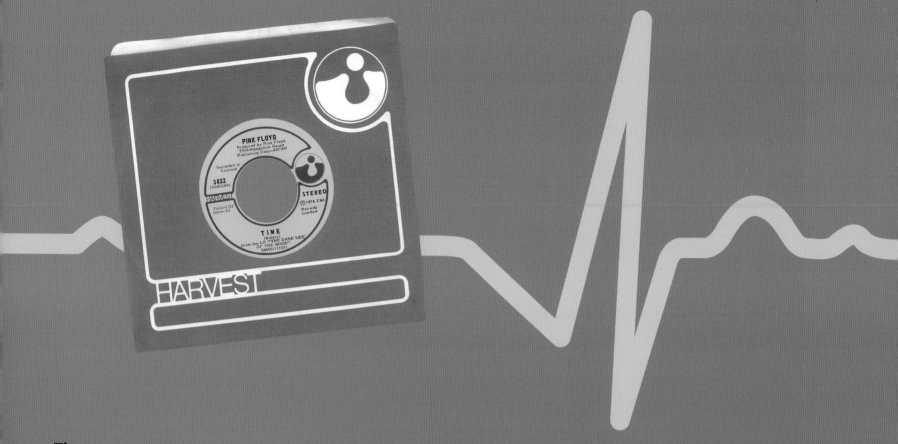

Time

There's a seamless transition from "On the Run" into "Time," the gauzy drift of it all destroyed by the sound of a dozen or so clocks going off, followed by the incessant ticking of a lone clock, metronome-like, the effect created by Roger plucking two different notes, muted, on his Fender Precision bass. In fact, Roger played to an actual metronome, which was placed in another room to isolate its sound from the recording, and then mic'd and fed to Roger so he could hear it—essentially a primitive click track. This is backed with an intermittent half-time heartbeat, which, 30 seconds before the explosion of the song into verse, goes full-time. Commenting across the beat is Nick using his four Rototoms tuned to the chord changes, mixed way back and echoey, with the top end somewhat blunted. The ominous chords during this section are accompanied by Rick, "commenting" like Nick, so to speak, using a Wurlitzer electric piano.

Pink Floyd in Marseille, France, where the band played five nights November 22–26, 1973, as part of a collaboration with the Roland Petit ballet company

American writer and transcendentalist Henry David Thoreau, who wrote "The mass of men live lives of quiet desperation," which is referenced in the lyric to "Time"

Rick is credited on this one along with the rest of the band (the last time this would happen), with Roger again writing the lyrics. Rick and Dave share vocal duties, Dave (aggressively, with an uncharacteristic hint of vocal fry) singing lead on the verses and the short reprise of "Breathe" added to the piece (sometimes separated out as "Home Again"), while Rick sings co-lead with Dave on the bridges. Additional to Dave and Rick is a quartet of female backing vocalists who add a lush sense of grandeur at the bridge.

"Time" becomes a conventional song after a couple minutes of the above-described sound collage, remaining so for the rest of its nearly 7-minute duration. It's quite rocky, with Dave throwing in chunky, funky chords and bendy Joe Walsh licks while Rick similarly slashes his way through the song on his Farfisa, along with strong, slightly distorted synth chords. Halfway through, Dave peels off a distorted, electric guitar solo, although like the Rototom "solo" earlier, he's rendered somewhat echoey and gauzy amid the mix—Gilmour performed this at sort of live high volume, improvising through his effects pedals into a Hi-Watt amp. After an extended blow there's a chord change and his lines get lyrical, augmented by a return of the bridge's backing vocal array. A second verse finally arrives, followed by a bridge, followed by a complex chordal transition to the "Breathe" reprise, for which Nick slows the tempo.

Lyrically, Roger hits us directly and in plain language with an admonishment about wasting time, waiting for life to happen, ending his initial berating with the graphic image of missing the starting gun. What follows is more devastating wordage that cuts to the bone, more on the theme already pressed upon us with words in "Breathe," and with sounds on "Speak to Me" and "On the Run," although here there's more of a sense of lethargy.

But soon it's back to the futility and meaninglessness of cramming in too much, as Roger uses words like "run" and "racing" and "shorter of breath." There are plans that implode, scribbled lines unused, and all the while the heart beats, again, sometimes slower, sometimes faster, always without meaning. "Quiet desperation" is referenced as "the English way," even if the famous quote from which it originates—"The mass of men live lives of quiet desperation"—comes from Henry David Thoreau, an American. To be fair, Roger does say "hanging on in quiet desperation," which indeed reflects more of a sense of the British "stiff upper lip."

PINK FLOYD

THE DARK SIDE
OF THE MOON

 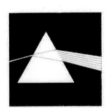 

A Superb #1 Gold Album SMAS-11163
With A Superb New Single,
"Money" (#3609)

And
A New Tour

June 15	Buffalo, N.Y. (Memorial Aud.)	June 23	Detroit, Mich. (Olympia Stadium)
June 16	Jersey City, N.J. (Roosevelt Stadium)	June 24	Cuyahoga Falls, Ohio (Blossom Music Festival)
June 17	Saratoga Springs, N.Y. (Saratoga Performing Arts Center)	June 26	Jonesboro, Geo. (Lake Spivey Park)
June 18	Rain Date for June 16	June 27	Jacksonville, Fla. (Vet. Mem. Col.)
June 19	Pittsburgh, Penn. (Civic Center)	June 28	Miami, Fla. (Pirates World)
June 20, 21	Columbia, Maryland (Merriweather Post Pavillion)	June 29	Tampa, Fla. (Tampa Stadium)

For all of Roger's nihilism, come the "Breathe" reprise, he hints at a sense of meaning. Across a redolent eight lines that could have been written in the Dark Ages, Roger speaks of a manual laborer, perhaps a farmer, who rests his bones by the fire, contemplating the toll of the church bells across the field. The implication is that the work may have changed over the centuries (or indeed, that the toil of centuries ago still exists), but the same questions of occupation and idleness and spirit persist.

The Great Gig in the Sky

The last track on side one began life as an organ piece from Rick and on the original record is credited to Rick alone, constituting his fourth credit out of five songs on side one. It was intended as a commentary on religion; thus, the early working titles "God," "The Religion Song," and "The Mortality Sequence." Bolstering the effect, early live versions included snippets of Bible passages and dialog from church sermons, although at one point the guys tried dialog from NASA astronauts.

In its final form, the song begins with bass, unadorned piano, and drums, but then gathers a head of steam, with Nick playing forcefully and with organ parts added by Rick. The song lived for a long time as an instrumental, but then vocalist Clare Torry was called in, providing the legendary wordless vocal that evokes gospel singing (hence the retention of the original religious mandate) but also a sort of dramatic death throe, both roiling concepts reflected richly in the grand titling. For her performance, Torry first tried singing some words, basically variations of an orgasmic "Oh baby," but was then told they would prefer it wordless. It was Torry's idea to picture her voice as an instrument. She was also told it was a song about dying. Galvanizing the concept is a smattering of on-theme spoken word. Putting a slight twist to this thematic framing, Roger has said the song addresses the universal fear of death, which he wanted to explore on the album, but again, preferably without lyrics.

And that was it for side one of *The Dark Side of the Moon*, clocking under 20 minutes of music with three of five selections being essentially instrumental. And yet so much is said, most pertinently—indeed devastatingly—through Roger's lyrics, but also through so much wordless music that is at times ruminative to the point of hypnotic—and at other times, nightmarish and promoting mania.

Music Hall in Boston,
Massachusetts, May 4, 1972

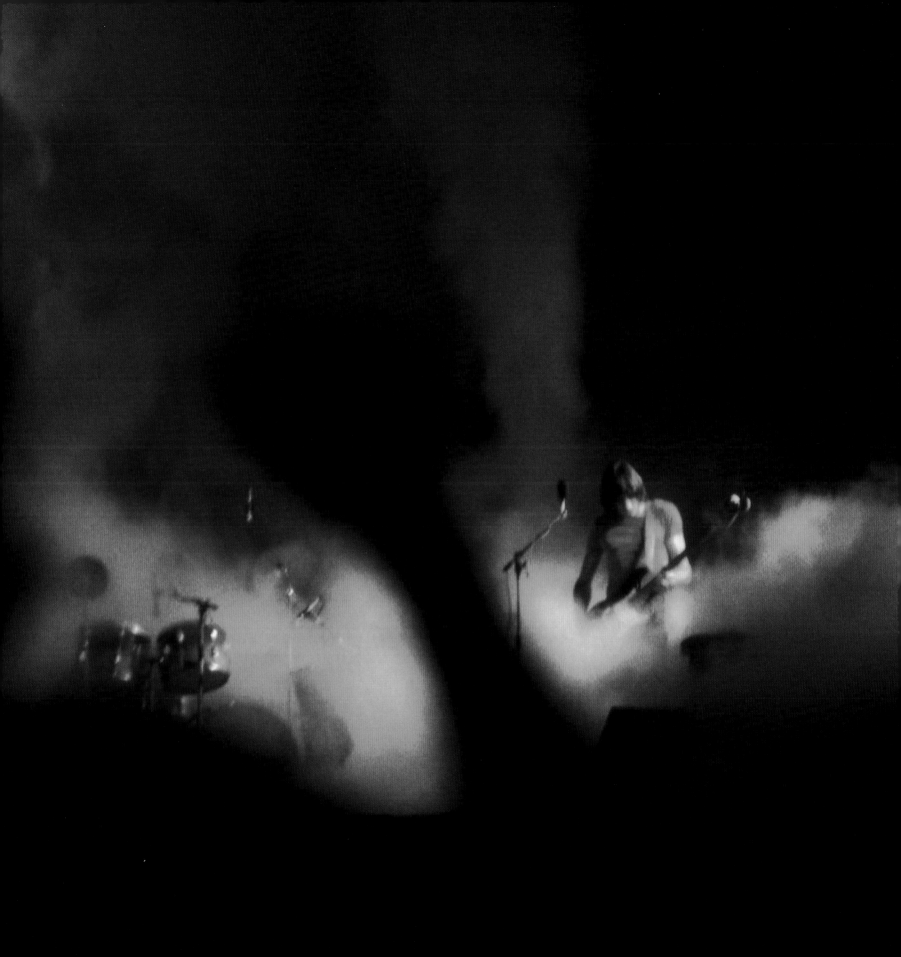

DAVID GILMOUR

David Jon Gilmour was born where Pink Floyd was born, namely that seat of higher learning, Cambridge, England, on March 6, 1946. His father, Douglas, was a professor of zoology at Cambridge and his mother was a schoolteacher and later a film editor at the BBC. An ardent student of the birth of rock 'n' roll in the mid-'50s, Gilmour was soon learning the guitar and buying records, already exchanging ideas with Syd Barrett in his early teens.

Enrolled in language studies in college, Gilmour persisted with the guitar and in 1962 joined a band called Jokers Wild that recorded, at Regent Street Studio, an EP, configured as a one-side, five-track album. Jokers Wild played a party in Cambridge in 1965 that also had Pink Floyd on the bill and Storm Thorgerson in the crowd. (Paul Simon was there as well and jumped on stage and did "Johnny B. Goode" with David's band.)

Into the summer of '65, Gilmour busked around Spain and France and at one point had to be hospitalized for malnutrition. The last straw came on a subsequent trip to Paris in mid-1967 when, playing there with members of Jokers Wild, first as Flowers and then as Bullitt, the band had their equipment stolen and the promoter refused to pay them. Broke and back in London, Gilmour was present when Pink Floyd recorded "See Emily Play" and by the end of the year he was asked to join the band.

Over the years in Pink Floyd, Gilmour settled into the roles of guitarist, co-lead vocalist, and co-composer. He's viewed as the most musical member of the band and the supplier of melody through his lyrical guitar playing and his silky-smooth voice, the antithesis to Roger's cranky bark (although, mind you, Roger also has a gear that can compete with Gilmour for plush accessibility). Gilmour's solo in "Comfortably Numb" from *The Wall* is often cited as the greatest guitar solo of all time, if an artform so small (and so plentiful in the world) could be said to be ranked. Between *Animals* and *Wish You Were Here*, David released a solo album called *David Gilmour*, which got to #29 on the Billboard charts and was certified as gold. Playing bass on the album was Gilmour's old band mate in Jokers Wild, Rick Wills, soon to enjoy great success as part of Foreigner.

Power struggles and arguments over direction resulted in what was assumed to be a breakup of Pink Floyd, but to Roger's surprise, Gilmour had decided he was going to carry on with Floyd—and not with Roger. But the first order of business for David would be another successful solo album, *About Face*, issued March 5, 1984. This album also went gold in the US, thanks to regular radio play of the zesty "Blue Light" and plush ballad "Love on the Air."

The Gilmour-led Pink Floyd would be good for two hugely successful albums and similarly epic tours, but outside of that, David's music-making would be sparse, with Gilmour gaining a reputation as a semi-retired country squire living at his farm in Sussex. Indeed, in 2003, he was made a Commander of the Order of the British Empire. Gilmour also picked up an expensive hobby, becoming a pilot and a collector of historical airplanes. Bottom line, later in life he often seemed not much of a music guy.

But David would make a comeback as a solo artist, issuing in 2006, *On an Island*, a star-studded affair but all David in temperament, typically cozy and light, slow of tempo, sometimes orchestral, often atmospheric, occasionally rocked-up. There was also *Rattle That Lock* in 2015, more of the same melancholy, most of the lyrics once

again by his (second) wife since 1994, Polly Samson. Add in some substantial touring, a couple live albums, and DVDs, and suddenly there was a David Gilmour cottage industry, despite remarks over the years that framed Gilmour as the perfect example of a rock star acting dignified in his advancing years (and enormous wealth) by keeping quiet.

To sum up Gilmour creatively, Pink Floyd in the '80s and '90s confirmed that he was who you thought he was when the band was operating in the stratosphere, throwing down thunderbolts from a gunmetal sky. And then

the solo career—four consistent and utterly nonaggressive records spanning five decades—confirmed doubly that David Gilmour was who you thought he was previously in those different versions of one of the biggest bands in the world.

Pink Floyd's final (quasi) album is called *The Endless River*. Well, that's David Gilmour in Pink Floyd and outside of it, a river of music, both as unremarkable and unnotable as the dependable river flowing through a small town, but also as subtly magical, life-giving, and transfixing.

DAVID GILMOUR

A SOLO ALBUM FROM
DAVID GILMOUR OF PINK FLOYD

SHVL 817 ALSO AVAILABLE ON TAPE

ROGER WATERS

George Roger Waters was born September 6, 1943, in a village in Surrey, England, called Great Bookham. He was the younger of two boys born to mother Mary and father Eric, who had been a schoolteacher, Communist Party member, and a conscientious objector, setting up the son for a lifelong defiant political streak.

Also affecting Roger deeply, when he was but five months old, his father was killed in World War II, having changed his stance and joined, only to be killed at the Battle of Anzio, February 18, 1944. Following Eric's death, Mary moved the family to Cambridge, just north of London, which was soon to become a cultural capital of the world at exactly the time that it would matter most to the guys in Pink Floyd.

In school, Roger was good at cricket and rugby but also, by fifteen, he was a nuclear disarmament activist. Post–high school and enrolling at the Polytechnic-Regent Street (now University of Westminster) in architecture, the rebellious Roger soon fell out of his studies and into a life of music. After a debut record with Pink Floyd dominated by the writings of Syd Barrett, Roger took over control of the band, aiming to take it in a direction "more political and philosophical." However, the following clutch of albums essentially found the band spreading the wealth, with new guitarist David Gilmour pretty much judged to be the best singer of the lot.

The Dark Side of the Moon represents Roger's coming-out party in terms of defining the creative vision of Pink Floyd. The concept was his but at any point, one imagines that any of the other guys could have jumped in. Instead, Roger wrote all the lyrics for the album, is most prominent of the four in the music credits, and, perhaps telegraphing a bumpy power struggle across the ranks, is the lead vocalist of choice at the back end of the track sequence, singing the last two songs.

Roger would write virtually all the lyrics and sing the majority of the songs across four very successful Pink Floyd albums to follow (even playing a bit of guitar) before an acrimonious breakup of the band after *The Final Cut*, the album upon which Waters' dominance became a point of public record, with history essentially framing it as the first Roger Waters solo album. The album brings into full view a recurring theme addressed sporadically through the catalog, namely the futility of war, with *The Final Cut* addressing Roger's loss of his father as well the Falklands War and Great Britain under Margaret Thatcher and the Conservatives.

With Floyd continuing part-time after Roger's departure, Waters went to work building what became a succinct four-album solo catalog, well regarded but always in the shadow of the brand along the way. First came *The Pros and Cons of Hitch Hiking*, quickly after *The Final Cut*, in the spring of 1984. The title track would become a bit of a radio staple, pushing the record toward RIAA-certified gold status, although it would take another eleven years to get there. Next came complicated concept album *Radio K.A.O.S*, which garnered a #50 placement on Billboard but never managed gold certification. This was followed by *Amused to Death* in 1992, perhaps Roger's best-reviewed album, which got to #21 on the Billboard charts, driven up the grid by the hit status of "What God Wants, Part I." Finally, there's *Is This the Life We Really Want?* from 2017, in this writer's opinion a masterpiece of golden-period Pink Floyd proportions. But nobody cared, other than a small army of Roger loyalists.

What the general public *did* care about was Roger celebrating his legacy, which he did in bombastic, deafening fashion, this parallel second career dwarfing then drowning out any parlor-room pontification over the solo canon. It all began on July 21, 1990, when Roger mounted an epic performance of *The Wall* in Berlin to commemorate the fall of the Berlin Wall eight months previous. Conservative attendance estimates were pegged at 200,000 with upward of a billion watching on TV. The double album documenting the event was certified platinum in the U.S.

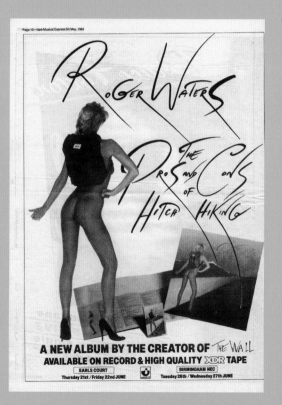

In 1999, twelve years since mounting an actual tour, Roger embarked upon the *In the Flesh* campaign, which started small and then sold well, requiring venue upgrades and an extension that became three years. In 2005, Roger put out an opera album called *Ça Ira*, following up his work on an operatic treatment to portions of *The Wall* the previous year.

Since then, Roger has settled into a life as one of the biggest and most successful touring acts on the planet, with elaborate shows heavy on Pink Floyd and, in particular, *The Wall*. Through dogged determination and force of persona, he's become at least equally Floyd as Floyd if not more so, especially during all the many years when the brand was on the shelf.

Roger's late-in-life reputation has been diminished by some due to his outspoken views on Israel and its treatment of Palestinians. As is the nature of the argument, the more vociferous the stance, the more one is accused of antisemitism, and Waters has not escaped such vitriol. He is an ardent supporter of the Boycott, Divestment and Sanctions movement (BDS) and regularly advocates for the movement's goals, namely the cutting off of all financial ties to Israel as a means toward what he sees as a more equitable situation for the Palestinian people. Despite this being the narrative that seems to stick to Roger, he's been outspoken on myriad other political and economic issues over the years, again exhibiting a consistency of character borne into him since, really, in childhood and with the death of his father, who, as Waters framed it, was betrayed by politicians' promises of a postwar dream society that never came.

Roger thumps his Fender Precision somewhere in the Netherlands.

5 Side Two

"When at last the work is done"

Money

Us and Them

Any Colour You Like

Brain Damage

Eclipse

Side two of the original *Dark Side of the Moon* begins with the record's outlier in every way, from its uptempo music through to its time signature and even lyric, not to mention the fact that it was far and away the most successful song from the record as a single, reaching #10 in *Cashbox* and #13 on the *Billboard* singles chart.

On tour in America,
spring 1973

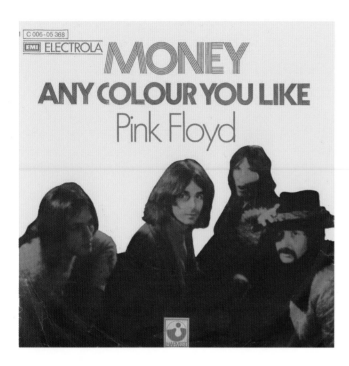

Picture sleeves for the German
(above) and Danish (opposite)
issues of "Money" b/w "Any
Colour You Like"

Money

As Pink Floyd's first U.S. Top 40 hit ever, "Money" served as the gateway drug to the rest of the album. Subsequently, most of the songs—all of them less fun but also prettier—could be heard on classic rock radio forever after.

"Money" is credited to Roger alone, so it's not surprising that the bass is central to its being—even if his loping riff is doubled with guitar, albeit nearly inaudibly. But first there's a stunning and geometric sound collage of coins and cash registers, carefully built with actual measured and spliced tape to play out atop a 7/8-time signature grid, gorgeously captured with effects alternating into hard right and left pans with sounds up the center as well. Reinforcing the timing of the sound effect piece is the doubled bass and guitar riff, then Nick's swinging, shuffling drums—snare on two, four, and six—lightly graced with Wurlitzer electro piano from Rick and color-commentary guitar from David, who also provides the surly, energetic, and bluesy lead vocal, captured in a couple of takes. The overall effect is of a complicated point-counterpoint weave, vaguely in a reggae zone. And as with good progressive rock, the casual listener soon finds the 7/8 meter smoothing out in one's head to the point where it stops being confusing and instead becomes the song's pleasurable hook.

Still, the biggest hook is the stunning opening sound effect, so good they bring it back later. Also notable is the lengthy saxophone solo from Dick Parry, again, played for maximum hook for the casual listener, and becoming one of the most recognizable rock 'n' roll sax solos of all time. And if you don't like sax, Wright and Gilmour are cooking up some maximum funk; Rick playing like Billy Preston on a Stones record while Dave politely plays rhythm, periodically cutting through with the famed tremolo effect he gets out of his Kepex processor.

Next comes this not very rocking record's rockiest moment, where a loud wind-up announces a shift into a 4/4 swing, atop which Gilmour solos loudly on a Stratocaster. What's amusing is that although everything's changed around him, Rick can still play his funky wah-wah organ part. This muscular swing section soon gives way to a quiet blues breakdown,

PINK FLOYD

6C 006-
05 368

MONEY

ANY COLOUR YOU LIKE

THIS PAGE: Sleeves for the French (left) and U.S. (below) issues of "Money" b/w "Any Colour You Like"

OPPOSITE: Roger Waters, Olympia Stadium, Detroit, Michigan, June 24, 1975. The first two verses of "Us and Them" resonate strongly with Roger's family story.

everybody crouching, Roger muting his walking bass line, as Dave continues to solo. You'll notice that there's a continuous two-fisted high-hat part here necessitating Nick's tom-tom performance to be stuck in as an overdub. Then it's back to full steam ahead, Dave higher up the fretboard on his Lewis guitar now and Nick beginning his bar-ending fills earlier but still playing simply, his notes wide apart, with many of them on the toms. There's a couple more verses—amusing, the band is playing the song faster now—and another go-'round of what serves as a chorus. This is followed by a lock onto a 4/4 version of the verse music and some spoken word and we're done.

The "Money" lyric is a bit of an anomaly, taking us away from the deep life-and-death introspection of what came before, with Roger, ever the Labour activist, casting scorn on greed and materialism. The link, however, is that the pursuit of riches is part and parcel of the empty frantic activity alluded to on the first side of the album. Then it's over in a blink.

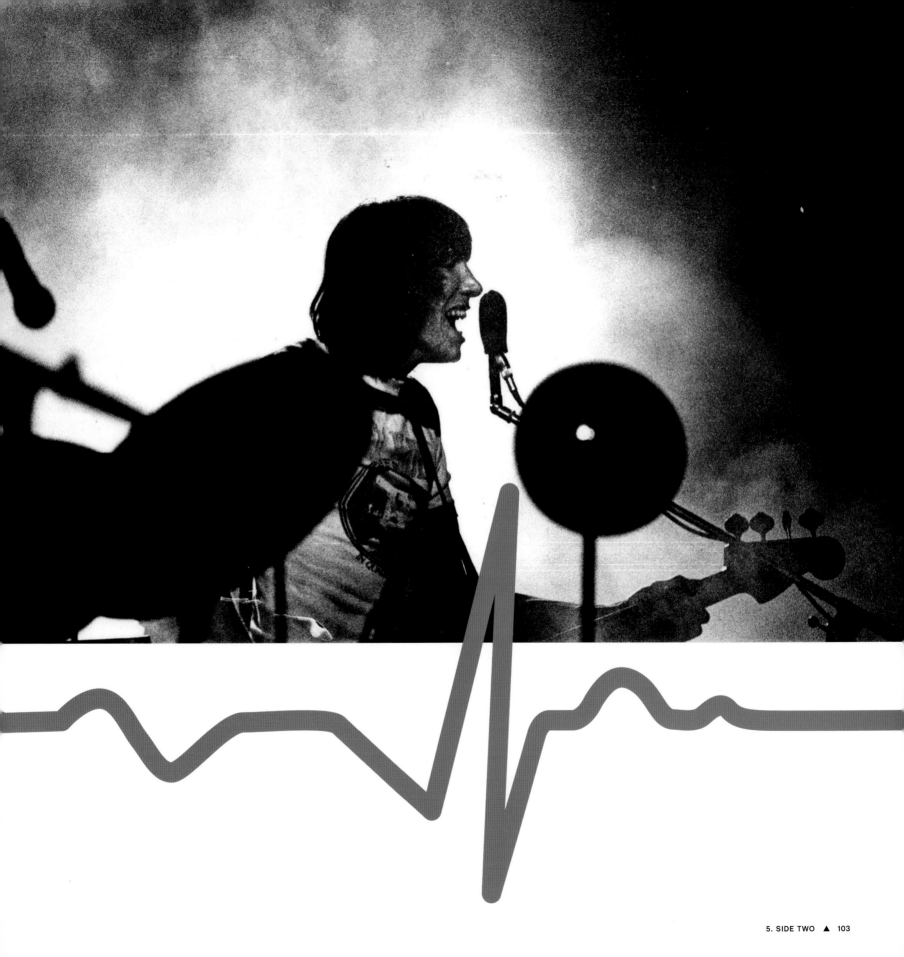

Us and Them

The next track on side two of *The Dark Side of the Moon* represents a second somewhat political song on the record. In fact, Roger's themes here of war, racism, protest, and poverty—a lot of territory covered across a typically spare set of lyrics—would gain in prominence and preoccupation in later years, most pertinently on *Animals*, *The Final Cut*, and arguably three of his four solo albums. In fact, one might say that the rift between David and Roger over the literary themes of the band begin here, in tandem with the germination of the operational power struggle between the two.

But the music isn't by either of them; rather, it's Rick once again, writing a slow ballad even deeper into a dream-like state than "The Great Gig in the Sky" (also his) or "Breathe (In the Air)," which had him writing with David. The idea comes from something he had written as soundtrack music back in 1969 to be used in the movie *Zabriskie Point*, which came out the following year. Director Michelangelo Antonioni rejected the music at the time, called "The Violent Sequence," as too sad and churchy. A reworked version of the band's "Careful with That Axe, Eugene" was used instead, leading to Rick's solo piano piece languishing and getting revamped into this stoner rock classic!

As the song opens, everybody is playing the softest rock possible, with a returning Dick Parry on saxophone playing smooth jazz. There's no sharpness to any of the performances, with the drums mixed distant, echo and reverb everywhere, with the only notes not washing like waves coming from Parry and occasionally Rick, who weaves in the odd church organ flourish—his instruments of choice on this one are a Hammond organ and a Steinway piano. It takes 1:44 of the song's 7:49 (it's the longest song on the album) before we hear a vocal, at which time David croons "Us," followed by an echo of the word. Then comes "and them," followed by an echo of "them." This seems innocuous now, but in 1973 it took some ingenuity getting the repeat to work in "forever" Pink Floyd time. Parsons used a 3M eight-track machine on the side, with two tracks repeating at a time, in pairs. Dolby units were also utilized, all in the successful attempt to place the echoes in different parts of the stereo spectrum.

ABOVE: "Us and Them" appeared on the B-side of the U.S. seven-inch release of "Time."

OPPOSITE: Rick in need of another beverage at the Sportpalast in West Berlin, June 5, 1971. "Us and Them" has Rick writing a ballad even deeper into a dream-like state than "The Great Gig in the Sky."

The verse ensues, set to the same music as the long intro, Roger's octave-jumping bass line floating us forward into the heart of the song. But then the clouds part and the music swells in strength, augmented by epic, vaulted background vocals, with Rick joining Dave on the leads, harmonizing. Even Dick Parry is back, and parallel to the lyrics reflecting Roger's personality, so too does the music sound like the arrangement methodology we'd hear one day from him on *The Pros and Cons of Hitch Hiking* and *Amused to Death*.

Lyrically, the first two verses resonate with Roger's family story, with soldiers (us) being sent off to war, as generals (them) watch from the rear. There's the vague sense of a chessboard to the presentation, with the orders coming from the back while the "front rank" dies in battle. A nice turn of phrase has the generals sitting while the lines of the map move side to side.

Next comes the "black and blue" verse that Roger has stated is about racism, followed by a verse about "civil liberties," Waters presenting a brief snapshot of a protest where a poster-bearer thinks it's a war of words, but is arrested all the same. Finally, a beggar on the street, for the lack of funds to buy a meal, dies because everybody is too busy with their own problems to drop him a few coins. All four situations feature a strong us-and-them dynamic and the musical setting is one of surrender, capitulation, and resignation that nothing is going to change any time soon.

As for the music, what ensues is further oscillation between the sublime verse structure and the positively grandiose choral section (for lack of a better term), with Parry pervasive in the mix and even taking a solo section. This is also the song in which Roger the Hat tells his road rage story, all while Rick tinkles away on his Steinway, taking Floyd dangerously close to easy listening.

"Us and Them" backed with "Time" was issued on February 4, 1974, as the second single from *The Dark Side of the Moon*, non–picture sleeve, in Canada and the U.S., both edited down to half length. The song peaked at #84 in Canada, and #72 in *Cash Box* and #101 in *Billboard* in the States.

Nick onstage at Olympisch Stadion in Amsterdam, May 22, 1972. Mason took co-writing credit on "Any Colour You Like," which began life as a jam with Dave and Rick.

Any Colour You Like

The third track on side two represents continuity with side one by serving as the second side's only instrumental piece, even if it's less of a sound collage and more of a progressive rock jam. It also bisects the second side of the original vinyl between things out in society and things in the world that might drive one mad—in this sense, "Any Colour You Like" is the sound of the brain deconstructing, of synapses declining.

The track was cooked up late in the process as a jam on two chords, kicked off with the synth "to set the mood," said Nick, and is credited to him and Dave and Rick. It's also sometimes called "Breathe (Second Reprise)" due to the similarity of chord sequence (or more like quantity of chords and chord changes). In the main, it serves as a showcase for Dave (who Parsons calls the true synth wizard in the band) and the VCS 3 synthesizer, with Gilmour executing short loops and long echo (also, Rick plays some Hammond). It also serves as a showcase for the album's high-fidelity characteristics, with fans hearing these cutting-edge synthesizer sounds for the first time and then playing them to their friends at high volume as they roll a joint on the gatefold. Additionally, Dave gets to solo, highly treated and psychedelic through a harmonizing Uni-Vibe effect and throbbing tremolo, utilizing spinning Leslie cabinets to add to the marijuana-enhanced ear-candy nature of the song. Playing the song live, the band would often stretch the jam out well beyond its official 3½ minutes before collapsing into the payoff guitar line and vocal of "Brain Damage," which signals the beginning of the album's near apocalyptic endgame.

As for the title, Roger's told the story of hawkers selling pottery out of the back of a truck, cajoling prospective housewife buyers, "You can have any color you like; they're all blue." Waters then goes on to reflect on blue being the dark side of the moon as well as the bright side, and good and evil, with all of it being the same color. Then there's the story of Pink Floyd road boss Chris Adamson, who used to quip, when asked for a guitar, "Any color you like . . . they're all blue."

Amsterdam Rock Circus, 1972. "Any Colour You Like" is a showcase for the loops and echo Gilmour executed with the VCS 3 synthesizer.

Inherent in this also is the idea of choice and freewill, as addressed elsewhere on the album thus far, in terms of going to war, being faced with consumerism, and even with respect to being born. Indeed, also salient is the idea of fear of committing to life choices—there's no question that a sense of panic has been instilled across the likes of "Breathe," "Time," "Money," and "Us and Them" that feeds into this confusion about where to go next. What's more unsettling is that perhaps an even greater sense of anxiety has been conjured by the songs with no lyrics at all.

Brain Damage

As we wind toward the culmination, we arrive at the penultimate slot with "Brain Damage." One of the original songs played just after the end of the *Meddle* tour, "Brain Damage" had the working title of "The Lunatic Song" (or "Lunatic") and also "The Dark Side of the Moon," underscoring its anchoring to the album that would make Pink Floyd pop culture titans. What's more, being about Syd Barrett, it was equally the blueprint for *Wish You Were Here*, a collection of classic rock radio staples just as seminal to rock 'n' roll history creatively speaking, if not as much with the accounting

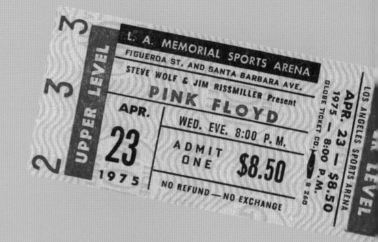

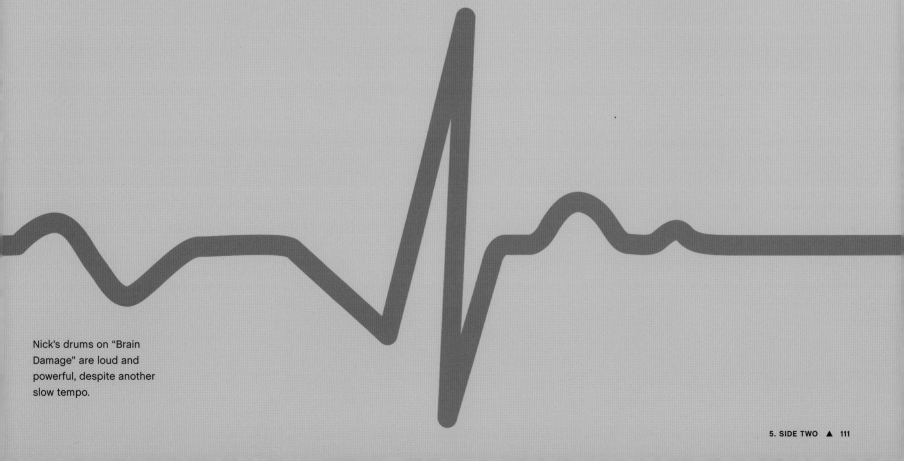

Nick's drums on "Brain Damage" are loud and powerful, despite another slow tempo.

ABOVE: The band performs at Amsterdam Rock Circus at the Olympisch Stadion, May 22, 1972. Gilmour's Bill Lewis guitar can be seen leaning against his amp.

OPPOSITE: Waters has explained that meeting on the dark side of the moon can be an invitation to communicate about what you're going through.

class. In finished form, here "Brain Damage" sits, possibly the greatest song on the record, as crafty, confident, and climactic as any moment on *The Wall* or your favorite 4 minutes from "Shine On You Crazy Diamond."

As the song begins, Nick keeps time with high-hat as Dave picks a refreshing bit of Beatles-esque guitar—and there's that heartbeat. Roger begins to sing, for the first time on the album, on a song that is all his. It's not the caustic Roger we will meet later, however; this is Roger singing like Dave, and double-tracked for maximum smoothness.

But what he's saying is much more harrowing than the Waters wonderings from earlier on the album, bleak as they were. To be sure, the opening salvo from "Brain Damage" sounds very much about a case of lunacy close to home, namely Syd, with mention of the grass (as Roger specifies, the square between the river and King's College Chapel, but with the meaning also tied up in the double entendre "Please keep off the grass"), plus "games and daisy chains and laughs," which sounds fully Syd. But we must remember that the album is about the pressures of life causing lunacy, and so there's a sense of "There but for the grace of God go I," with Roger intimating that any one of us is just a couple of life challenges away from having their head cave in.

There's a great turn of phrase where Roger pictures the newspapers as full of lunatics, but as a sort of protective measure, the papers can be turned over, their faces pressed to the floor (for some reason, I can't help but picture the cover of Syd's *The Madcap Laughs* album when I read this). Next comes the identification with insanity, described as a dam breaking "many years too soon," rising to the titular words, "I'll see you on the dark side of the moon."

The music at this juncture is as grand and "heavenly" as the loud bits on "Us and Them," once more making use of backup singers Lesley Duncan, Doris Troy, Barry St. John, and Liza Strike, who go beyond the preceding wordless vocalizing to the point of actually singing the lead with Roger. All the while Rick presses down hard on the album's most extreme and churchy version of Hammond organ yet, and Nick's drums are loud and powerful. But what can you do with another slow Pink Floyd tempo? Not much. In other words, Mason's fills are his typical spare clumps of toms; fortunately, at the sonic end, they sound better than ever.

Album closer "Eclipse" is a swirling cauldron of performance and volume. The band plays Detroit, 1975.

As for David, his two main functions throughout are the "Dear Prudence"–like picking of the verse along with the sighing high slide notes played on lap steel—the acoustic-style picking (but on electric) is part of the loud bit but is pretty much drowned out by the bravado playing of Rick and Nick, not to mention the cavalcade of vocals.

Then we're back to another verse, where a lobotomy is taking place—brain damage to repair the brain damage—and of course it doesn't work, with the subject locked away permanently, tormented by the fact that what's in their head is no longer them. Here's where the "found sounds" idea with the spoken-word bits is most unsettling, given the spliced-in laughter from road manager Peter Watts.

With the final deluge of gospel music, we're back to what sounds like the description of an acid trip, resulting in a point-blank statement about being in a band that is now playing different tunes. This can refer to two things: one being that, as Syd degraded, there were instances where the band would play a song but Syd wouldn't fully join in or perhaps even play something else altogether; and two, the heartbreaking observation that Syd would have to watch as a band for which he once wrote all the songs suddenly was out there in the world playing different songs. A third related layer of meaning is the idea that a band you were once in is humankind or society, and suddenly everybody is coalescing on a shared melody different than the one rattling inside your damaged brain.

But once again, Roger comforts the lunatic (again, *luna*, moon), promising a reunion on the dark side of the moon, which, as before, can be read two different ways: as a place of shared insanity or beyond the veil into the shadow lands, into death. And yet offering a ray of hope—hope of repair or at least communion—Waters has explained in interviews that meeting on the dark side of the moon can mean, essentially, let's communicate about what you're going through (with an admission from my end that I have the same psychological slippage), the point being that you're not alone.

The song sighs to a close with another round of the verse music with only snippets of chatter and Rick on modern crazy-making EMS VCS 3 synthesizer.

Eclipse

The Dark Side of the Moon draws to a close with "Eclipse," which serves, curiously, to make the chorus passages of "Brain Damage" feel like pre-choruses, with this new, similarly gospel-arranged music in 6/8 time serving as the bombastic, late-arriving chorus to a longer piece, rather than a self-contained song of a modest 2 minutes. The swirling cauldron of performance and volume, with the descending chord sequence and Rick firing off Hammond B3 licks and Nick bashing his cymbals, find Pink Floyd creating a version of soul music, also conjured during "Us and Them" and "Brain Damage" but now more theatrical, as the brain receives the signal that the guys are about to wrap things up with a big red bow. Roger begins singing short lines in a sort of listing pattern and is soon joined by the backing vocalists, underscoring the southern Baptist vibe of the big closing number before the preacher shakes hands and sends everybody home. As the music ends, we're back to the heartbeat, which inevitable has to stop.

At the lyric end, we're back to one of the themes of "Breathe," namely that "All you touch and all you see is all your life will ever be." But stop the presses: there's not the same negativity. Instead, after the detailed summation of a life lived, fully twenty-five line items (that long a list alone is a reason to keep living), Roger tells us that it's all "in tune." Unfortunately, he doesn't stop there, though (if he did, he wouldn't be Roger Waters). In what renders the above a sort of false ending, for the very last line of his lyric, Roger draws the dagger, telling us that even the mighty sun, the life force, is eclipsed by the moon, by death.

But even that is a crafty false ending of sorts.

Before we go, Roger mischievously slides in Gerry O'Driscoll's "There is no dark side of the moon, really; matter of fact, it's all dark," which Waters viewed as a spot of levity, a bit of a "man behind the curtain" moment, with someone of no particular flash standing in the world summing up life in a tossed-off quip, while the geniuses in Pink Floyd worked months on the answer and perhaps, in the end, missed the point, if the Abbey Road doorman is to be believed. The final kicker, after this flurry of false bottoms, of panicked valuations and reevaluations, is that O'Driscoll's assessment of the world turns out to be even darker than Roger's.

RICK WRIGHT

Richard William Wright, born July 28, 1943, in Hatch End, Middlesex, England, got involved with the Floyd guys, namely Roger and Nick, in architecture school at the Polytechnic-Regent Street. Recovering from a broken leg at age twelve, Wright taught himself a number of instruments but began concentrating on the piano at his mother's suggestion. Curiously, in Sigma 6, his first band with Roger and Nick (and classmate Clive Metcalf), Rick would play piano if one was available at the pub they were playing, but otherwise go for trombone or guitar. Wright then switched from architecture to music school, took a sabbatical and went to Greece, and then returned to London, where his position solidified as keyboardist in Pink Floyd.

Early on with Floyd, Wright was considered the most qualified musician in the band, writing and arranging, occasionally singing, tuning guitars and basses, and even hauling the gear. But as time went on, Wright found himself disinterested and even depressed as his marriage deteriorated and Roger came on like a steamroller creatively. Credited on five *Dark Side of the Moon* songs and the dominating "Shine On You Crazy Diamond" cycle from *Wish You Were Here*, Rick had zero credits on *Animals* and by the time the guys were trying to build *The Wall*, where Rick also wrote nothing, Roger wanted him out of the band. Subsequently, Wright did not tour the album, nor would he appear on *The Final Cut*.

But it would be Roger who was gone in time for the next Pink Floyd album. Rick would return for *A Momentary Lapse of Reason*, but as one of many session keyboardists, listed third in the credits in a smaller point size than David and Nick, who were the only band members pictured. He'd be back again as a full member come *Division Bell*, co-writing on five tracks and providing lead vocals on "Wearing the Inside Out," even though he noted in the press that contractually he was not on par with David and Nick. Further strengthening his status, Wright toured with Floyd from here on out and appeared on the *Pulse* live album, issued in 1995.

Outside of Floyd, Wright was good for an album called *Identity* from Zee, a duo he formed with Dave Harris from Fashion. He also saw issue in 1978 of a solo album called *Wet Dream*, and, in 1996, a second and final solo project called *Broken China*, presented as a four-part concept album about his wife's battle with depression.

Rick Wright passed away from lung cancer at his home in London on September 15, 2008, at the age of sixty-five. By the end, he had been through three marriages, fathered three children, and outside of England had lived in Greece, France, and on his yacht in the Virgin Islands. He was also a full-fledged member of Gilmour's touring band and had been in the throes of working on a third solo album.

Pink Floyd's final project, a double album of mostly ambient and instrumental music called *The Endless River*, was presented as a tribute to Rick Wright. Underscoring the sentiment, a track therein called "Autumn '68" features Rick playing the pipe organ at the Royal Albert Hall back on August 26, 1969, preparing for a show later that evening.

"WET DREAM" OF RICHARD WRIGHT OF PINK FLOYD.

A NEW SOLO ALBUM ON COLUMBIA RECORDS AND TAPES

"Columbia," 🔊 are trademarks of CBS Inc. / © 1978 CBS Inc.

NICK MASON

Nicholas Berkeley Mason, born January 27, 1944, in Birmingham, England, cobbled together his first set of drums around a pair of bongos and a few bits and pieces at age fourteen and was off to the races—literally, as we shall see later. Mason, like Roger and Rick, fell out of architecture studies into Pink Floyd and never looked back.

Nick is the only member of the band to appear on every album and play on every tour. In terms of songwriting, he is well-represented in the early days, with a diminished showing on *Dark Side of the Moon* and then not appearing again until *The Endless River* in 2014. His key credits include "Interstellar Overdrive," "A Saucerful of Secrets," "One of These Days," "Echoes," "Speak to Me," "Time," and "Any Colour You Like."

Nick's love of motor racing was born early, with his father, a documentary filmmaker, working on films about racing when Nick was in his teens. Mason in fact races himself, utilizing many of the classic cars in his extensive collection and having competed in the 24 Hours of Le Mans. Mason has owned over forty Ferraris throughout his life, with the 250 GTO he bought in 1977 for £37,000 now being worth over £40 million. Nick has written three books on auto racing, as well as a memoir in 2004 documenting his time with Pink Floyd. He also flies helicopters and is part owner of the Bolton Wanderers Football Club.

Outside of Floyd, Nick has issued one solo album, in 1981, called *Nick Mason's Fictitious Sports*. All the songs were written by Carla Bley, who also plays keyboards, while the vocals are performed by Robert Wyatt from Soft Machine. He's also done a

NICK MASON

FICTITIOUS SPORTS

Nick Mason of Pink Floyd delivers his first solo album 'Fictitious Sports.' Featuring Robert Wyatt, Carla Bley and Chris Spedding

Album & cassette TC/SHSP4116

series of soundtrack projects with 10cc's Rick Fenn. Mason is famous for having produced *Music for Pleasure*, the second album for punk band The Damned, issued in 1977 (as the story goes, the band asked for Syd Barrett and were given Nick), as well as Gong's sixth album, *Shamal*, issued the previous year. Considered a conciliatory link between Roger and David, Nick has appeared live as a guest with both gentlemen as they go about their business as solo artists.

In recent years, Nick has enjoyed a surprise musical renaissance of sorts, having embarked on effusively reviewed tours beginning in 2018 as Nick Mason's Saucerful of Secrets, documented in a delightful live album from 2020 called *Live at the Roundhouse*. The band's mandate is to perform songs from Pink Floyd's psychedelic era, which they do brilliantly. As well, like David (but sixteen years later), Mason was made a Commander of the Order of the British Empire, presented the award by Prince William.

6 The Tour

"And if the band you're in starts playing different tunes"

The *Dark Side of the Moon* campaign proper began in Madison, Wisconsin, three days after the album hit the shops.

Of course, the songs were now closer in construction to the record compared to when they were played live throughout 1972—the band got them tight at full production rehearsals at the Rainbow Theatre on February 19–21, 1973. There was now a twenty-speaker quadraphonic sound system in place plus new film collages, as the band hit the road working solidly through March in the eastern and the southern U.S., plus a couple of shows in Canada, both in big hockey arenas. For the first time the band consistently used extra performers on stage. Playing sax was Dick Parry, who also appeared on the album, plus three backup singers from Leon Russell's entourage, namely Nawasa Crowder, Mary Ann Lindsey, and Phyllis Lindsey.

Another key change would be a switch in front-of-house sound engineer from Chris Mickie, who took care of things in 1972, to Alan Parsons. Parsons had been a pioneer in quad sound and done some of that on the album; now here he was steering his own oil tanker of quad. Unfortunately, working in quad caused a bit of a kerfuffle, when the album's quad mix wasn't completed in time for the launch party.

Dark Side of the Moon
Tour, Winter Gardens,
Bournemouth,
January 22, 1972

On February 27, press had been gathered to hear the new opus at the London Planetarium, but the band—except for Rick—boycotted the event, represented instead at the gala by life-sized cutouts. Had they shown up, the guys would have been incensed, with the stereo version of the album played through a decidedly non-hi-fi system arranged by EMI.

Keeping tabs on the much better sound system on the *Dark Side* campaign was Peter Watts, who also handled this job in '72, with the legendary Arthur Max serving as overall production manager and keeper of the increasingly sophisticated lighting system, assisted by

Robin Murray and Graeme Fleming. Watts had been with the band for years after having tour-managed for Pretty Things. He's famed for his spoken-word contributions on the album but, unfortunately, would leave the Pink Floyd fold the following year and die of a heroin overdose in 1976, with the band providing financial support to his family after his passing. Max, a New Yorker who also worked Woodstock, would go on to a famed career as a film production designer. Tour managing was Mick "The Pole" Kluczynski.

The *Dark Side* songs had been shifted from their 1972 position at the beginning of the set list to the back half of the show, before the encore. Set one for the first few shows in March was "Echoes," "Obscured by Clouds," "When You're In," "Childhood's End," and "Careful with That Axe, Eugene." Mid-March, "Echoes" was moved to the end, with "Set the Controls For the Heart of the Sun" replacing "Childhood's End." Then came all of *Dark Side* in order, followed by "One of These Days" for an encore.

The band departs for a twelve-day tour of Japan, March 3, 1972.

吹けよ風、呼べよ嵐

ピンク・フロイド

'72 3月6日(月) 7日(火) pm6:30
東京都体育館

S・¥2,800 A・¥2,500 B・¥2,100 C・¥1,600

★都内各プレイガイドにて好評発売中!!
★お問い合せ (585) 3045 ユニバーサル

主催● フジテレビ
　　　 ユニバーサル
後援● 東芝音楽工業
協賛● 平凡パンチ
　　　 アン・アン

The New York City show at Radio City Music Hall on March 17 was considered a bit of a showcase, with all manner of press and rockstar, as well as Andy Warhol, making up the crowd of 6,000. The band went on at an ungodly 1:30 a.m., rising from elevated platforms at the rear of the stage while vents near the front of the stage gushed pink smoke.

April was taken off, with the tour's homecoming party set for Earls Court in London on Friday, May 18 at the Exhibition Hall, the occasion being a benefit concert for the National Campaign for the Homeless. A second show was added for May 19 after the first show quickly sold out, with the band playing to an estimated 18,000 fans on each night, valiantly battling the venue's notoriously boomy acoustics with their new quad system. Singing backups were Liza Strike and Vicki Brown, mother of future Floyd backup singer Sam Brown. The set list on both nights was the same as the one performed in the U.S. in late March. Highlights included Nick's gong being lit on fire (this also went down a storm in New York), a dry-ice waterfall for "Echoes," and the band crashing a 6-foot-long silver-and-red plane on wires into the stage at the end of "On the Run."

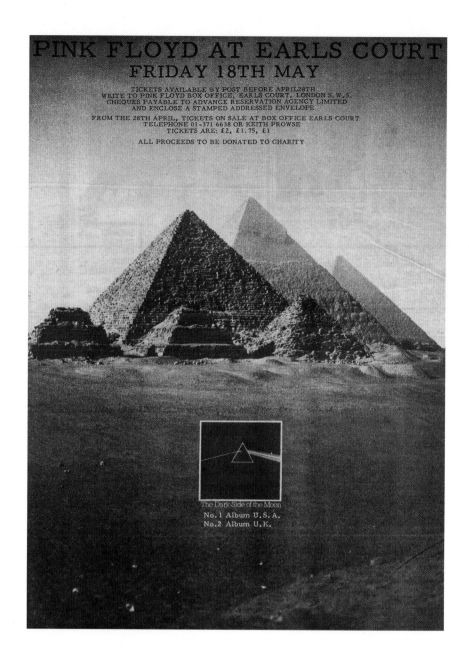

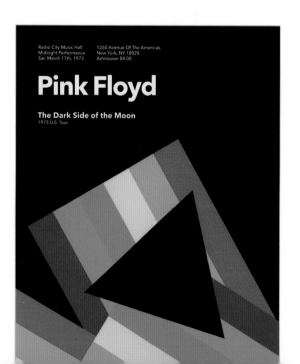

ABOVE: April 1973 was taken off, with the tour's homecoming party set for Earls Court in London on May 18.

With the album hitting #1 on the *Billboard* charts and "Money" going Top 20, the band returned to the U.S. for the back half of June, playing a mix of arenas and stadiums. The June 18 show at Roosevelt Stadium in Jersey City set a record for the venue, with the band grossing $110,565 in ticket sales. There were no shows from July through to mid-October, with the band playing Munich on October 12 and Vienna on October 13. Assisting during these two shows was a backup singing troupe consisting of Billie Barnum, Venetta Fields, and Clydie King. The storied trio had been much in demand individually over the years and had come together as the Blackberries at the behest of Steve Marriott of Humble Pie. Dave asked Humble Pie drummer Jerry Shirley if they could be borrowed for the two shows; Shirley, a pal of Dave's, passed the request on to Marriott who reluctantly said yes. Fields, along with a new Blackberry, Carlena Williams, would sing with the band live in 1974. Both feature on Pink Floyd's next album, *Wish You Were Here*, issued in 1975.

The mainland European concerts were followed by two shows at the Rainbow Theatre in London in November, a benefit stand that raised £10,000 for former Soft Machine drummer and singer Robert Wyatt, who had been paralyzed from the waist down after a fall out of a fourth-floor window. Singing backup were Vicki Brown, Liza Strike, and Clare Torry, who performed her iconic part in "The Great Gig in the Sky."

There'd be no new Pink Floyd album in 1974, but the band toured, essentially extending the *Dark Side of the Moon* campaign. First would be seven dates in France in June, recorded for broadcast by Europe 1 radio. It marked the first time the band used their signature circular projection screen, known moving forward as "Mr. Screen." All of *Dark Side* was still being played, along with "Shine On You Crazy Diamond" and an early version of *Animals* song "Sheep," called at this point "Raving and Drooling."

Next came an extensive U.K. campaign in November and December to close out the year, with the November 16 show from Wembley's Empire Pool in London (the third of four in a row at the venue) recorded by BBC Radio One for broadcast. "Echoes," featured in set one in France, was moved to the encore position, with an early version of *Animals* song "Dogs," at this early stage called "You Gotta Be Crazy," closing out the first set. The British dates saw the introduction of a comic book-format tour program called *The Pink Floyd Super All-Action Official Music*

TOP: The Blackberries, Venetta Fields and Carlena Williams, provided backing vocals on the 1975 North American tour.

ABOVE: The band played at two benefit shows for Robert Wyatt (pictured) at London's Rainbow Theatre on November 4, 1973.

A comic book–format tour program called *The Pink Floyd Super All-Action Official Music Programme for Boys and Girls* featured art by Gerald Scarfe (above), who would take on a greater role with *The Wall*.

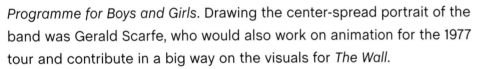

TOP RIGHT: Olympia Stadium, Detroit, Michigan, June 1975

BOTTOM & OPPOSITE: Memorial Sports Arena, Los Angeles, April 1975

Programme for Boys and Girls. Drawing the center-spread portrait of the band was Gerald Scarfe, who would also work on animation for the 1977 tour and contribute in a big way on the visuals for *The Wall*.

A light 1974 bled into a light 1975, with tensions rising as the band felt drained of creativity and nervous about how to follow up the masterpiece that was *The Dark Side of the Moon*. The limited gigging the band saw in 1975, in April and June in North America with a lone outlier, Knebworth on July 5, felt like a further fixation—to the point of obsession—upon the record from 1973. To be sure, the entirety of *Dark Side* was still performed every night, but as a ray of hope, good chunks of the band's next two albums also got an airing on a daily basis. If this novel idea of road-testing so much new material could work once, surely it might again.

As it turned out, the guys were not wrong.

LIVE AT POMPEII

As French philosopher Paul Valéry (or English poet W. H. Auden, depending on your source) once said, "A work of art is never finished, merely abandoned." *Live at Pompeii* apparently wasn't finished *or* abandoned when it limped into limited view September 2, 1972, because it rose to life again in 1973, expanded, now successful, and part of the magic *Dark Side of the Moon* story.

The scene of the Adrian Maben–directed concert film was the ruin of the Roman-era amphitheater in Pompeii, with the band set up in the middle surrounded by a profusion of prog rock gear, ready and willing to take us on a trip into their *Meddle* album and much more. The film also found the band playing live with no audience, other than a few local children allowed to watch on, no doubt horrified at what they saw and heard. Having the place empty was a deliberate gesture and experiment by Maben, who posed the arrangement as a sort of anti-Woodstock, solemnly focusing the viewer on the enveloping music without the distraction of crowds shaking all over.

As for the odd venue, Maben had lost his passport on a previous holiday to the ancient volcano-buried city and found himself wandering the stone ruins looking for it. It seemed like a good idea to film Pink Floyd there, given both were creepy and quiet and all about ambience—and meaning. A steep stipend was paid to the city to allow the place to be molested by the arriving hippies, who played a nightmarish set there over four days, October 4–7, 1971, recorded on a mobile eight-track unit brought in from Paris.

Captured quite violently were "Echoes," "A Saucerful of Secrets," and "One of These Days," each dramatic and bombastic, with the sessions really presenting Nick Mason in his finest hour, headbanded, hirsute, surrounded with toys. Added to the Pompeii performances were songs recorded at Studio Europasonor (a TV soundstage) in Paris on December 13–20: "Careful with That Axe, Eugene" (as insisted upon by Maben), "Set the Controls for the Heart of the Sun," and "Mademoiselle Nobs," an impromptu slow blues featuring a dog howling away with the band as a sort of reproduction of "Seamus" from the *Meddle* album. The showcasing of Nick continues through the French footage, but all told, each Floyd member gets his due, with Maben capturing the band across these two sessions—sunny and dark—exquisitely, augmenting the near relentless drama with psychedelic footage, historical stills, and shots of flowing lava and waterfalls, resulting in an action-packed work, despite the band's very psychedelic flight path. Also, the camera work and editing are excellent, featuring close-ups and cross fades and always sensible transitions—*Live at Pompeii* is a very professional early-days concert film, even if the subject matter (Pink Floyd as *Meddle*-makers) is considerably distant from what mainstream audiences might want.

Unsurprisingly, *Live at Pompeii* didn't make much of a dent on pop culture consciousness upon release in 1972, with critics finding it pretentious and kind of a bummer, given its lack of an audience and therefore crowd response. But that all changed after the smash success of *Dark Side of the Moon*. Maben had already expressed reservations, while out flyfishing with Roger in early 1973, that the film was too short at 1 hour and in need of some padding. The result was critical rock history being captured, with Maben taking a 35 mm camera to Abbey

Adrian Maben directs the band at Studio Europasonor in Paris, December 1971.

Road to document the creative process as the band went about building what, at the time, was just another Pink Floyd album, destined for the usual mild troubling of the charts. Subsequently, the version of the film reissued in late 1973 included music from "On the Run," "Us and Them," and "Brain Damage," along with quite a bit of band banter as they studiously pieced together what would turn out to be, much to everyone's surprise, one of the monumental albums of not just the '70s, but of all time.

After its Montreal debut in November 1973, the new version of the film, at 80 minutes, slowly found its way to U.S. audiences throughout 1974, grossing by October of that year $2 million in box office receipts. Still, Pink Floyd's priority in 1973—and 1974 and 1975—was the record, with *Live at Pompeii* remaining, at the time, a curio. Its very real effect has been felt over the decades (especially when viewing was made easy by the internet), offering two key things over the years. First, we see a snapshot of the band wild an' free pre–*Dark Side*, incendiary hippies making a lot of noise, obsessed artists making their mark on the world. Second, the film preserves images inevitably burned into the brain with respect to what it was like making *The Dark Side of the Moon*. We see the guys young, animated, energetic, and competitive, as with the preposterous Pompeii stand, pouring themselves into their art and also hanging out in the lunchroom. Only this time they're not making *Meddle*— it's *The Dark Side of the Moon*. This, ultimately, is the significance of *Live at Pompeii*. Because of these captures, it is no less than the band's version of Peter Jackson's *The Beatles: Get Back*—in similarity hugely revealing of personality, in contrast magically fleeting.

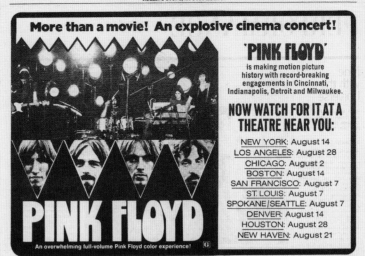

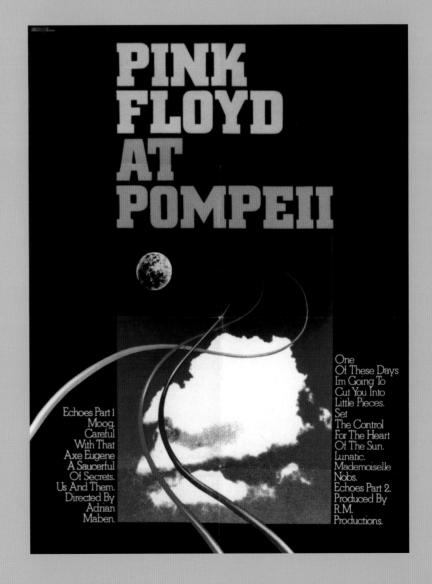

FLOYD'S NEW U.S. DEAL WITH COLUMBIA

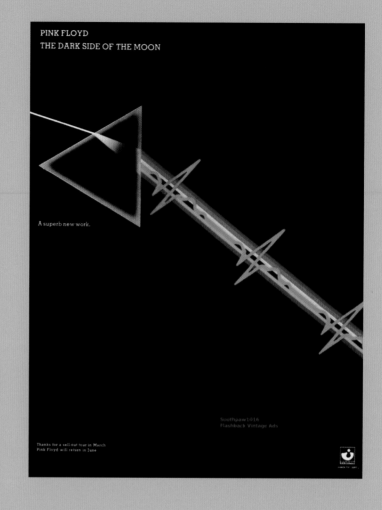

If it looked like Pink Floyd and EMI were having a grand ol' time together for all those years and all those records, behind the scenes there was subterfuge. Well before *Dark Side of the Moon* came out, making the band a household name, Clive Davis had been busy raising the reputation of American CBS imprint Columbia Records, signing the likes of Donovan, Bruce Springsteen, Blue Öyster Cult, and Aerosmith. Davis had become president in 1967 and worked to convert the imprint from a respected pop and jazz label to a rock label, jumping in with the pysch bands and later championing quadraphonic sound.

As for troops on the ground, key was A&R rep Kip Cohen, who had been keeping an eye on Pink Floyd, having become acquainted with them when he was managing Bill Graham's Fillmore East. Cohen was instrumental in getting the label into negotiations with Floyd manager Steve O'Rourke. It seems the band was not happy with the promotion and attendant results EMI had been getting up through *Obscured by Clouds*. One of Davis's savvy moves was bringing O'Rourke to one of Columbia's sales meetings, where staff talked strategies for the latest singles. As a result, in early 1974, just as *Dark Side of the Moon* came out, Pink Floyd had already flown the coop, although they would remain an EMI/Harvest band back on

home soil. With the deal came a reported $1 million advance, and for the first time the Floyd guys had some money. But there was no more Clive Davis—he had been fired back on May 29, 1973, due to allegations of financial improprieties, and was replaced in 1975 by Walter Yetnikoff. The implication is that the courting of Pink Floyd goes back at least to early 1973.

Little did either party know that it would be two years before they would have their first project together. There was also the awkward situation of EMI suddenly working a massive hit record with the band, one in

which one of Floyd's complaints, a previous lack of fancy packaging, had been assuaged, given that *Dark Side of the Moon* came with two posters and two stickers. What's more, EMI seemed to be doing a pretty good job of promoting the album, due to newly appointed chairman Bhaskar Menon taking an interest in the band, vowing to do better than the label had done with *Meddle*. As a result, EMI had planned edited versions of songs for singles, giving them the best shot at radio, and had spent large sums on advertising.

Still, once in America, everything could look quite different. O'Rourke had been

imprint called Columbia, which had nothing to do with Columbia in the States, having split off and become part of EMI with the American Columbia becoming part of CBS (and later Sony). Also of note, the new Columbia deal encompassed the world outside of the U.K. and mainland Europe, with the most notable territories besides the U.S. being Japan, Canada, and Australia. This is, more or less, how the arrangement would stay, right up through the Roger-less years until *The Endless River* in 2014.

OPPOSITE: EMI seemed to be doing a pretty good job of promoting the album, due to newly appointed chairman Bhaskar Menon taking an interest.

THIS PAGE: Early Columbia Records press photos for the band

impressed with the energy at Columbia's Manhattan offices versus the comparative lethargy at the iconic circular Capitol Tower in LA (Capitol being EMI's U.S. affiliate), where bands right there on the Strip got the attention—Pink Floyd Inc. could hardly have been further from sight—and mind.

With the EMI contract set to run out with the delivery of *Dark Side*, O'Rourke kept the Columbia negotiations quiet, not even allowing EMI to make an offer on resigning. Pink Floyd would be a Columbia act in America moving forward, with considerable success to follow, again, though, with EMI not only achieving success in the end but, in fact, selling and promoting what would be the band's biggest record ever.

Oddly, Pink Floyd's first five U.K. singles and three U.K. albums had also been released on "Columbia." However, this was an EMI

7 Sales and Awards

"Grab that cash with both hands and make a stash"

Pink Floyd enjoyed their first U.S. gold record, for American sales of over 500,000 copies, when the Recording Industry Association of America (RIAA) certified *The Dark Side of the Moon* on April 17, 1973, a quick six weeks after the record appeared in shops.

What followed was a long period when EMI gave up on counting copies, which corresponds suspiciously with the band leaving the label in the U.S. for Columbia. For the next seventeen years, there would be no more sales awards for *Dark Side*, meaning, conveniently, no more expensive audits and no need for awkward presentations from bosses you no longer work for (ascribing the lack of certification thusly is likely only partially true—EMI wasn't great at certifying Beatles albums during this period either). The RIAA introduced the platinum award in 1976 for sales of 1 million copies. Platinum for *Dark Side* would have to wait until February 16, 1990, however, at which time the record was certified eleven times platinum. (Diamond certification for sales of 10 million was not introduced until 1999.)

Roger Waters on the *Wish You Were Here* tour, 1975.

Check-ins on *Dark Side*'s numbers took place dutifully throughout the '90s, with the album adding another million in 1991 and 1994 and the record reaching fifteen times platinum on June 4, 1998. The Nielsen Soundscan system put in place in 1991 estimates 9,502,000 copies sold in the U.S. between 1991 and 2013, and the number settled upon for estimated worldwide sales at the time of writing is 45 million. This puts the album sixth all-time behind *Thriller*, *Back in Black*, the Whitney Houston–led soundtrack to *The Bodyguard*, *Bat Out of Hell*, and *Their Greatest Hits (1971–1975)* by the Eagles, who are nipping at Pink Floyd's heels on the list with a second smash seller, *Hotel California*, at 42 million happy customers (who can check out any time they like but can never leave).

Back home in the U.K., the album plotted a similar stratospheric arc, demonstrating that the band was about as popular there as they were in America (a correlation that is often not a given). The U.K. also has a silver designation, so it got there first, followed by gold near simultaneously and then platinum in 1976. Curiously, once more the certifications stopped until the album was designated seven times platinum in 1993 en route to its current status at fifteen times platinum, which it reached in late 2021. In 2017, it was pegged as the U.K.'s seventh highest selling album of all time.

In most other territories, *Dark Side of the Moon* is just a regular ol' successful album, with the notable exceptions being Canada, where it currently sits at double diamond (twenty times platinum, with platinum corresponding to 100,000 copies sold); Australia, where the album is officially fourteen times platinum; and France, where by 2015 it had sold approximately 1,715,000 copies, which puts the album at seventeen times platinum.

When streaming numbers are added in, it gets complicated, but *Dark Side of the Moon* holds its own, ranking eighth all time, behind, curiously, an almost completely different list of seven ahead of it than those stated above for physical sales, with total sales, including digital sales and full-album streams, coming to approximately 57 million.

The success of *Dark Side of the Moon* helped some of Pink Floyd's older records achieve certification. *Meddle* was the first to hit, reaching gold in October 1973, while *Ummagumma* was declared gold in February 1974. There'd be no more certifications for the hairy early-days noise-making records until 1994, with the first three albums, in fact, never even

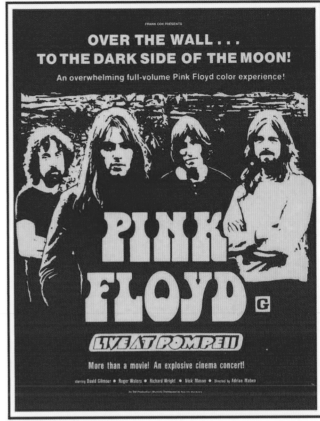

reaching gold in the States. Of note, all seven pre–*Dark Side* albums achieved some level of certification in the U.K. As well, in 2004, *Dark Side*-adjacent video *Live at Pompeii* reached double platinum in the video category for sales of 200,000 copies; three years later the Eagle Vision *Classic Albums* documentary about the record reached triple platinum. Nobody's bothered to check on potential certification for the record's singles in the U.S., but recent U.K. silver certifications were confirmed for "Breathe (In the Air)," "Time," and "Money."

FOLLOWING SPREAD: On tour in the U.S. in 1975. This was the beginning of a long period during which EMI had hit pause on counting sales of *Dark Side*. The RIAA hadn't yet introduced the platinum award for 1 million sales anyway.

ABOVE: Promotional sticker issued by Electrola in West Germany

OPPOSITE: The Floyd circa 1974—a band with a hit record

Underscoring the fondness that millions have for *Dark Side of the Moon* is the cavalcade of accolades it's received over the years beginning with a win in 1973 for album of the year as voted by the readers of British music weekly *Melody Maker*, beating out David Bowie's *Aladdin Sane*. It won a similar in *New Musical Express* the following year in both the British and world categories. Years later, in 2006, an *NME* readers' poll ranked it the eighth greatest record ever made (Planet Rock listeners shot it right to the top spot). Also on home soil, in 1997 *The Guardian* ranked *Dark Side of the Moon* #37 on a list of 100 greatest albums of all time. The album was also nominated for a Brit award, given by the British Phonographic Industry, in 1977, the very first year of the ceremony (The Beatles took the prize, for *Sgt. Pepper's Lonely Hearts Club Band*).

Although it has entered Grammy lore as one of the greatest snubs of all time, the album did get a nomination in 1973 for Best Engineered Recording, Non-Classical, the accolade essentially a credit to Alan Parsons. Making up for lost time, it received a Grammy Hall of Fame Award in 1998.

In 2020, *Rolling Stone* rated it #55 on their list of 500 Greatest Albums of All Time, a drop from its #43 place in 2003 and 2012. Additionally, it won a Q Classic Album award in 2014, with the Smashing Pumpkins' Billy Corgan presenting the award to Nick Mason. Q has considered it the greatest progressive rock album of all time (while prog-heads debate whether it's a prog album at all), as has *Rolling Stone*. In the big thick book department, the third edition of the influential *All Time Top 1000 Albums* series from Colin Larkin had *Dark Side of the Moon* at an exalted #9 following a poll of over 200,000 votes.

Finally, the album was designated "culturally, historically, or aesthetically significant" by the U.S. Library of Congress and chosen for preservation there, joining the first Ramones album, for which the author of this book was asked to write the LOC's contextualizing essay—there couldn't be two more diametrically opposed rock 'n' roll records on the face of the planet.

David searches for the lost
chord on his Bill Lewis guitar.

Roger rocks his Fender Precision bass—and a John Denver tee—at Nassau Coliseum, Uniondale, New York, June 16, 1975.

The Dark Side Of The Moon

No. 1 Album:

New Musical Express Readers' Poll 1974
British Section
World Section

Melody Maker Readers' Pop Poll 1973
British Section
International Section

Sounds Readers' Poll 1974
British Section
International Section

Disc Top Albums 1973

Melody Maker Top Albums of '73

Now available on Harvest
"A NICE PAIR" – Pink Floyd's
first two albums,
"The Piper At The Gates Of Dawn" and
"A Saucerful Of Secrets,"
repackaged by Hipgnosis.
Double Album at the special price of £2.50.

Harvest SHDW 403

THE BILLBOARD 200

One of the more amusing statistics associated with *Dark Side of the Moon*—akin to the idea that in 1976 every suburban household was issued a copy of *Frampton Comes Alive!* by the local municipal government—is the fact that *Dark Side of the Moon* has spent 961 weeks on the Billboard 200, the most of any album by a wide margin.

Back in the spring of 1973, the album hit the middle of the grid at #95, climbing to #1 on March 28, where it lasted all of one week. Oddly, the obscure *Obscured by Clouds*, reflecting the goodwill built up by the band over seven mostly difficult but well-meaning records, got to an impressive #46 on the important industry chart. But, of course, Pink Floyd was about to go through the roof. Garnering two more #1's and a #3 along the way, the band, by July 1988, had witnessed *Dark Side of the Moon* spend 736 weeks on the chart.

A change in the rules, downplaying back catalogs in favor of new releases, saw the album essentially banished from the table from 1991 through to 2009. But when catalog sales were reincorporated, *Dark Side* reassumed its frankly never-diminished commercial impact. Second but far behind in backlist sales was Bob Marley and the Wailers' hits pack *Legend*, which despite getting an artificial boost when it was priced at 99¢ by Google Play, still tracked at a third to a half of *Dark Side*'s numbers. By 2015 the now forty-year-old Pink Floyd institution was

up to 917 weeks, hanging around the lower rungs of the chart but still selling a good 8,500 copies a week by one measure or another.

On and off the Billboard charts, in 2020 *Dark Side* crept back on at #193, bringing the total weeks on the grid to 950 and then eventually 961 at last count. As it stands, the album is still far and away the recordholder in this department, followed by *Legend* and then

Journey's *Greatest Hits*, *Metallica*, Creedence Clearwater Revival's *Chronicle: The 20 Greatest Hits*, Eminem's *Curtain Call: The Hits*, Nirvana's *Nevermind*, Guns N' Roses' *Greatest Hits*, Bruno Mars' *Doo-wops & Hooligans*, and Adele's *21*. Rounding out the next ten we have The Beatles with their own hits package, *1*, bringing us full circle to Abbey Road.

TEN DARK SIDE OF THE MOON COLLECTIBLES

Consider this more so a trawl through different categories, albeit with the excitement being with the full-length LP, given that very few singles were issued pretty much anywhere, aside from "Money." Most of the big numbers at auction come from the U.K. first pressing and the Japanese Mobile Fidelity version of the album. Take the pricing info with a grain of salt—these are single examples, compiled and reconciled from Valueyourmusic.com, popsike.com, and Discogs.com. Fact is, prices are changing all the time, and as with any market, there is paying too much and then there is getting a great deal, especially given the wildcard of condition. So yes, this is more of a random list of ten yummy items, curated for variety.

The Dark Side of the Moon U.K. LP, first U.K. Harvest SHVL 804 pressing, 1973, with solid blue triangle on label, silver lettering, complete with two posters and two stickers.

The most desired pressing is the U.K. first pressing, for which prices vary wildly based on condition. In book-collecting parlance, this is the "first edition." One of these went for $4,283 U.S. in December 2018, but they are widely available at many price points. Once you get down to about the $1,000 mark, you start seeing nice copies of the first U.S. pressing.

The Dark Side of the Moon, Original Master Recording, UHQR by Mobile Fidelity Sound Lab in red on cover, catalog #MFQR 1-017, silver band at top. Japanese half-speed pressing, numbered and limited to 5,000 copies, 1981. Super-virgin vinyl, dust-free and static-free inner sleeve, reinforced box packaging. Later we got the U.S. series with the yellow band at top. A copy of the Japanese version sold for $3,550 U.S. in January 2020, with other copies selling in the $2,800–$3,000 range.

The Dark Side of the Moon, Japanese EMI issue, 1978, featuring a live shot of the band from the *Animals* tour on the front. Pressed by Toshiba on black vinyl. Blue and white insert. Counterfeits exist on black and red vinyl. English lyrics insert. Catalog #HW-5149. These sell in the $2,000–$3,000 range.

The Dark Side of the Moon, U.K. quadraphonic 8-track tape, white cartridge, catalog #Q8-SHVL 804, 1973. Issued in cardboard sleeve featuring front-cover art. One of these sold in February 2019 for $780 U.S. One of the most collectible 8-track tapes of all time.

Dark Side of the Moon (no *The*) 7-inch promo EP, U.S., catalog #PRO 6746. Features "Time" and "Breathe (In the Air)" on the A-side and "Us and Them" and "Money" on the B-side. All tracks are mono. Label hype text on back of picture sleeve. Green and yellow Harvest label. These appear regularly and have sold for upwards of $300 U.S.

"Money"/"Speak to Me," Bolivian edition on yellow Odeon label, non–picture sleeve but in die-cut white company sleeve. Catalog #BO-1171. There is no shortage of Pink Floyd "Money" singles pressed in many variants in many exotic countries. This example isn't particularly good looking, but it's pricey, one selling for $1,400 U.S. in September 2019.

"Money," U.K. edition, one-sided on pink vinyl from 1982 in picture sleeve. Edited version of "Money." Promo only, with letter indicating limited edition of 1,000 copies. Catalog #HAR 5217, yellow and green Harvest label. A copy of a non–picture sleeve variant backed with "Let There Be Light" sold for £917 on eBay.

"Money"/"Any Colour You Like," Danish pressing in picture sleeve featuring ink illustration of the band playing live. On Harvest, catalog #6C 006-05368. Black and silver EMI/Harvest label, 1973. A copy attracted twenty-one bids on eBay and sold for $677.

"Time"/"Breathe," black and white Harvest label, French promo issue for jukeboxes, 1974, catalog #JB Har 600.169. Produced by Pathe Marconi. Non–picture sleeve. These can be procured for $20–$50 U.S.

"Time"/"Us and Them," Canadian 7-inch issued February 4, 1974, catalog #3832. Non–picture sleeve, standard green and yellow Harvest label. Pretty common and not pretty—and not expensive. The U.S. got the same single, also non–picture sleeve.

Japanese Bonus Track: Our eleventh and last collectible is the first CD pressing from Japan in 1983. These were produced by CBS/Sony in Japan for Toshiba-EMI (Toshiba didn't have a pressing plant yet) with the catalog #CP35-3017. Featured was a silver obi strip and a twenty-four-page booklet, although it was also sold without the obi, replaced by a gold sticker on the cellophane. A copy sold in September 2021 for $750 U.S.

8 Pink Floyd
Post-*Dark Side*

"Long you live and high you fly"

After the rousing success that was *The Dark Side of the Moon*, Pink Floyd, in a sense, lived out the self-fulfilling prophecy embedded in the record's messaging, succumbing to the pressure of trying to live up to their reputation as the geniuses steering a rock 'n' roll juggernaut.

Relations between band members would deteriorate precipitously, Roger Waters would go through a divorce, and the next record, *Wish You Were Here*, would be difficult in birthing due to a collective case of writer's block and then not toured. In fact, there'd be no live dates in the back half of 1975 or in 1976. *Animals* would be toured for just the front half of 1977, with no shows happening in either of the following two years. Come *The Wall*, the visual extravaganza got so huge that the band set up for multiple shows across three venues in 1980 and then just two venues in 1981, thirty-one remarkably theatrical concerts in all over two years.

And then there were three—Richard, Nick, and David backstage in Rosemont, Illinois, during the band's *A Momentary Lapse of Reason* tour, September 28, 1987.

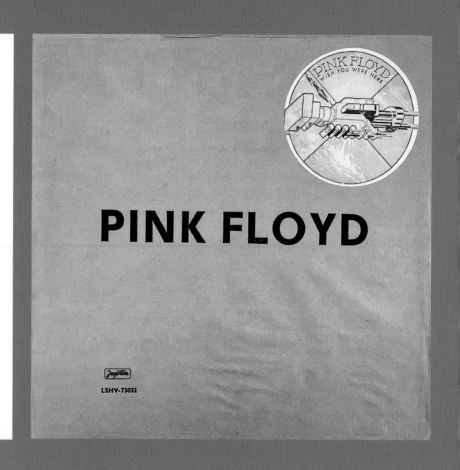

Still, the band managed to construct three creatively and commercially successful albums during this acrimonious period. *Wish You Were Here* was issued September 12, 1975, and sat at six times platinum in America at this writing. *Animals* was issued January 21, 1977, and is currently four times platinum. *The Wall*, a double album that pretty much singlehandedly rescued a moribund year of decline for the record industry, was issued November 30, 1975, and sits at twenty-three times platinum, although one can cut that in half for copies sold, given that each vinyl record counts twice.

Then comes *The Final Cut* in 1983, critically derided and commercially a let-down at double platinum. At this point there was barely a band behind it, and Roger was soon exiled to a solo career, with Rick, Nick, and David also silenced for a period, with the only musical bright spot being Dave's *About Face* solo album in 1984. The brand was revived, however, with an

ocean liner called *A Momentary Lapse of Reason*, arriving September 7, 1987, followed by an immense tour clear through to the end of the decade. The album has gone four times platinum, despite not a lot of lasting enthusiasm for the material, outside of the gorgeous first single "Learning to Fly" and its attendant stylish video, directed by Storm Thorgerson. A live album called *Delicate Sound of Thunder*, constructed from performances in August 1988, went triple platinum, underscoring the strength of the brand. Commendably, the band played most of the current album on tour; the inclusion of only a handful of *Dark Side* selections showed just how many classics the band had racked up over the years.

Clear through to 1994, the band would play but a couple of benefit shows, emerging full-throttle once again with a new studio album, *The Division Bell*, issued on March 28 of that year. The album currently sits at triple platinum in the U.S. with worldwide sales estimated at 7 million

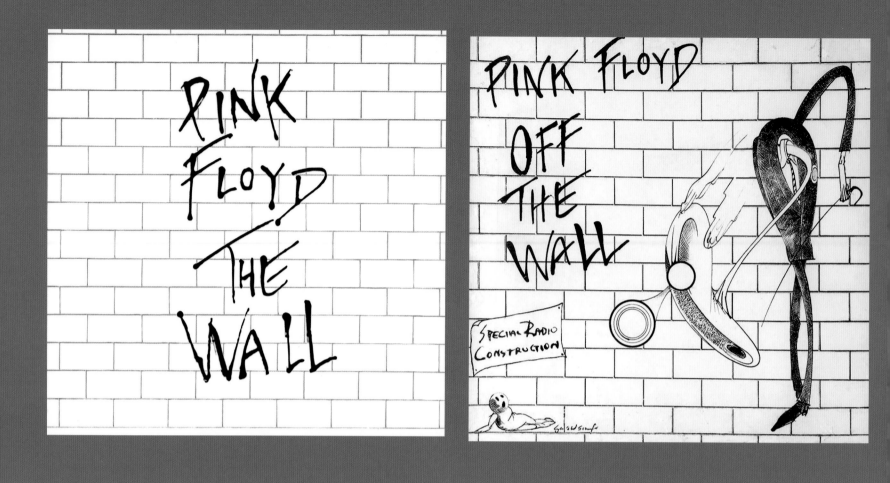

copies, its success fueled by a slate of dates in 1994 that saw the band tour intensively from March 30 through the end of October, with all the October dates being benefit shows performed at Earls Court. May 29, 1995, saw the release of the double platinum *Pulse* live album, notable for a performance of *The Dark Side of the Moon* in its entirety. Still, besides this tribute to the record most consider the band's greatest glory, Gilmour sculpted the live album around substantial chunks of the band's two most recent Roger-less records.

Poetically—but inescapably, painfully—the band would be good for but one more concert. On July 2, 2005, in Hyde Park in London, Rick, Nick, and Dave reunited with Roger to play Live 8, the follow-up benefit festival to 1985's Live Aid. It was their first show together since June 17, 1981, when the band had been at the height of its talismanic power, delivering the final Earls Court concert in support of *The Wall*. For the occasion,

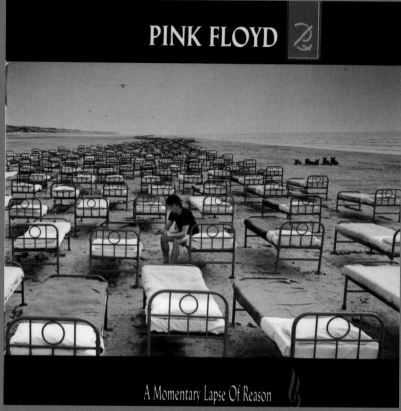

including three days of rehearsals, David and Roger tried to put years of acrimony (including very material legal battles) behind them. Indeed, the guys knocked heads over the set list, with David refusing to do "Another Brick in the Wall" and others, and battling Waters over the arrangements.

In the end, the band played "Breathe (In the Air)," "Money," "Wish You Were Here," and "Comfortably Numb," all but the last sung by Gilmour. At the end of the short set, it was awkwardly clear that Dave was having none of the warmth that Roger had desperately been trying to inject into the situation. It took everything in Waters' power to cajole Gilmour over for the arms-linked end-of-show bow, and it was apparent to everybody in the 205,000-strong crowd.

Post–Live 8, the band's catalog saw a boost in sales estimated upward of thirteen-fold. As well, the guys were offered a reported $150 million to

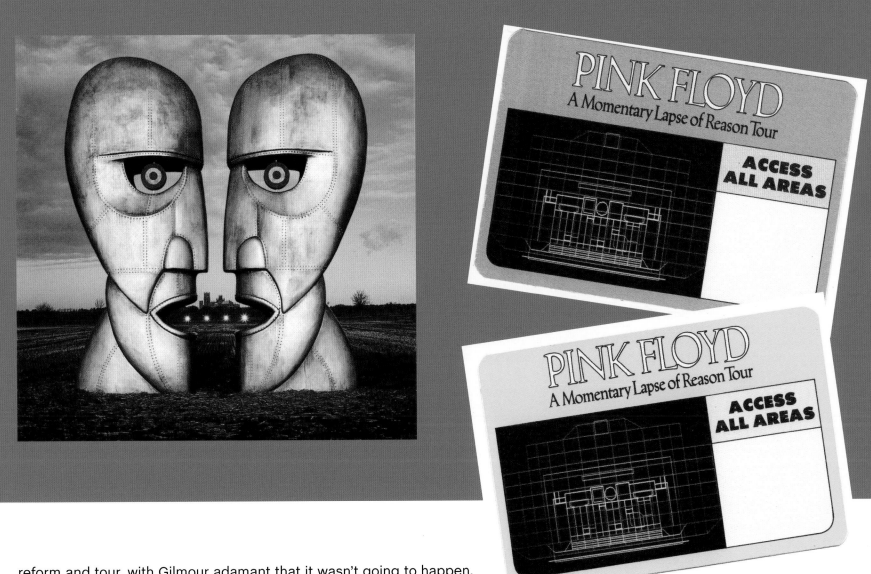

reform and tour, with Gilmour adamant that it wasn't going to happen, calling Live 8 "a one-off."

Not long after Live 8, Rick Wright passed away, putting an end to any such talk. And, indeed, the band never played live again, with or without Roger, partly due to the activity around Gilmour's *On an Island* record, his first solo album in twenty-two years.

If Live 8 represented something of a tidy dénouement to Pink Floyd as a live experience, the band's final album, *The Endless River*, did not. Mostly an ambient affair, the double album was positioned as a remembrance of Rick and is entirely instrumental save for one song, called (ironically) "Louder Than Words." The album makes use of synthesizer and keyboard parts Rick had left before his death from cancer, but that's not to say there isn't a lot of Nick and Dave all over the record, with many of the

ABOVE RIGHT: David, Nick, and Rick (and no Roger) accepting their Rock and Roll Hall of Fame induction, January 17, 1996

OPPOSITE: A reunited Pink Floyd at Live 8, Hyde Park, London, on July 2, 2005

compositions, frustratingly, resembling proper songs just waiting for a dreamy Gilmour vocal to be glazed over the top.

And if we thought they were done, on April 8, 2022, Dave and Nick and Pink Floyd adjunct bassist Guy Pratt reconvened for a benefit single called "Hey, Hey Rise Up!" in conjunction with Nitin Sawhney and Andriy Khlyvnyuk from Ukrainian band BoomBox. Gilmour and Mason created this "Pink Floyd with" song in support of the Ukraine Humanitarian Fund. David's official statement read, "We want to raise funds for humanitarian charities, and raise morale. We want to express our support for Ukraine and in that way, show that most of the world thinks that it is totally wrong for a superpower to invade the independent democratic country that Ukraine has become."

Excepting *The Endless River* and "Hey, Hey Rise Up!," might we say that Pink Floyd drew to an end in significant embrace of the record this book celebrates? The record that absolutely transformed the band's career as fearless pioneers of the quirky, destined for a valiant life underground, into one of the most regal and regaled rock institutions of all time? Yes, we might, for the material on *The Dark Side of the Moon* provides half of

OPPOSITE CLOCKWISE: Nick powering Nick Mason's Saucerful of Secrets, Milan, Italy, September 20, 2018; Rick during the historic reunion stand for Live 8, Hyde Park, London, July 2, 2005; Yes, Roger means you. *The Wall Live* tour, Gothenburg, Sweden, August 17, 2013; Roger on a solo tour at a sold-out ScotiaBank Arena in Toronto, July 8, 2022

ABOVE: The last night of Roger's 2013 tour, September 21, in Paris

the band's final live album in 1995 and then half of the band's final set list ten years later, that night in 2005. What we've arrived at serves as a likely unwitting—and yet fully fitting—tribute to a record that continues to captivate generation after generation of rock fans asking the same large and universal questions posed across this timeless record now fifty years in the rearview mirror.

Beyond Gerry O'Driscoll's amusing assessment that "There is no dark side of the moon, really; matter of fact, it's all dark," there is indeed ample time and space for comfort and resolution after reflection upon the things said on *The Dark Side of the Moon*. Ultimately, in this light—prismatic, solar, or merely hoped for—it's very much assured that new and younger waves of believers in the magic of music will keep on finding solace—and maybe even a few answers—in *The Dark Side of the Moon* for many generations to come.

On April 8, 2022, Dave, Nick, and Pink Floyd adjunct bassist Guy Pratt (right) convened for the benefit single "Hey, Hey Rise Up!" along with Nitin Sawhney (left) and Andriy Khlyvnyuk (not pictured) from Ukrainian band BoomBox in support of the Ukraine Humanitarian Fund.

DARK SIDE OF THE RAINBOW

The concept is simple: if you drop the needle (or hit play) on *The Dark Side of the Moon* and simultaneously start the film *The Wizard of Oz* (also from the beginning) with the sound off, the Floyd album suddenly emerges as a soundtrack to the 1939 fantasy classic.

It's one of the first internet conspiracies ever, started on a Pink Floyd newsgroup in 1995 and then publicized further when Charles Savage wrote about it in the *Fort Wayne Journal Gazette* in August of that year. The idea spread in an old-school manifestation of viral, with Turner Classic Movies even getting into the game in 2000 and helping out with a synched airing of film and album.

Once the band heard about it, they laughed it off. Mason wisecracked that the album was actually synched with *The Sound of Music*. Alan Parsons went further, explaining that the idea was "a nonstarter," because the band wouldn't have had any way to view a movie in the manner required to do the job. Even if crude videocassette recording technology had been tinkered with for years, any machines available at the time of recording the album were rare (mostly in TV stations), with mass-market availability not beginning until 1975 and not picking up steam until 1979.

As well, various experiments readily viewable on YouTube show what happens when *Dark Side* is butted up against *The Godfather*, *The Shining*, and most splendidly, *Paul Blart: Mall Cop 2*. In fact, the No Nerd Allowed! YouTube channel worked out a mathematical formula to count the synchs—let's just call them what they are, synchronicities in the Carl Jung (or The Police) sense: "circumstances that appear meaningfully related yet lack a causal connection." Parallels between the album and *The Wizard of Oz* ranked middle of the pack.

And let's face it, "Speak to Me" and "On the Run" work with almost anything, and "The Great Gig in the Sky" and the heartbeats at the end of "Eclipse" are pretty amenable too.

As well, the mind tends to dispense with synchronicities that don't work. There are plenty of spots where there's much action and rushing about in the movie while Pink Floyd is doing their patented "most laid-back music ever recorded" thing, which of course comprises most of *Dark Side*.

Finally, where one begins the synch is up for grabs, complicated by both the opening title cards and the reverse fade-in of "Speak to Me." One paired-up version's highlights might be completely missing in another version, which suddenly has generated a whole different set of highlights.

Arguably the greatest lesson to be learned from all this is one that (suspiciously?) the Floyd had already learned and then utilized to great commercial success on the very album wrapped up in this *Wizard of Oz* business. And that's the idea that a layering of the unrelated, like snatches of conversation on top of Pink Floyd music, can result in astonishing creative synchronicities, magic moments of completely new artworks. It's a concept not dissimilar to the découpe technique of the Dadaists (and then famously practiced by William Burroughs and then David Bowie), which is the idea of physically cutting words and phrases out of magazines and jumbling them together to see what new images arise when this is stuck next to that.

So let's crack open this conspiracy: Pink Floyd were already telling us in code back in 1973 that *The Dark Side of the Moon* was really designed as a soundtrack to *The Wizard of Oz* through the actionable metaphor of Roger's cue cards full of questions. After all, are we really to believe that Alan Parsons and the guys, with all their synthesizer prototypes and pioneering work in looping and quadraphonic sound hadn't, along the way, cobbled together their own working version of a VCR?

IMMERSION BOX SET

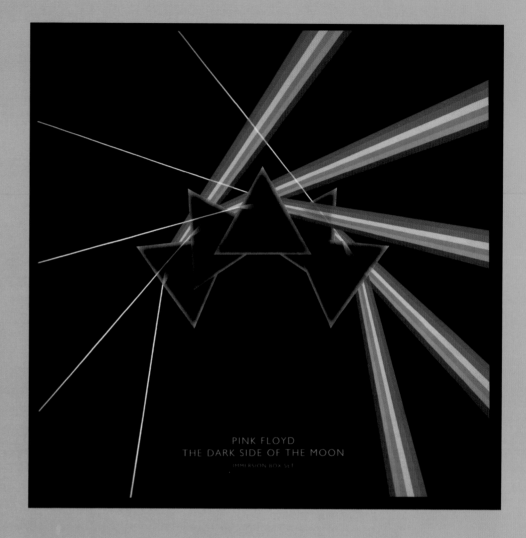

PINK FLOYD
THE DARK SIDE OF THE MOON
IMMERSION BOX SET

On September 26, 2011, EMI delivered the ultimate version of *The Dark Side of the Moon* in the form of the *Immersion Box Set*—at the current time, *Immersion* boxes exist for this album, *Wish You Were Here*, and *The Wall*, with a box full of *Animals* looming.

As a leading general statement, one would have to say that despite the raft of goodies enclosed, the package doesn't replace a vinyl copy from 1973 but rather reinterprets and expands upon it.

Beginning with the visuals, there's a sturdy box, festooned at the front with multiple prisms and refractions, aided in the effect by spot varnish. Inside, speaker grille–like foam keeps all the bits and pieces cozy, including, in order (arguably) of substance:

An anchoring booklet, forty pages stuffed with memorabilia shots and variants of the prism artwork. There's an essay about the graphics from Storm Thorgerson, a few credits, and the lyrics to the songs, one each per page. Conspicuously absent is any sort of liner essay about the album (but then again, fortunately, you've got this book).

A second twenty-four-page booklet is called *Pink Floyd on Tour 1972–74: Jill Furmanovsky and Hipgnosis*. Again, there's no context, no captions.

Rounding off the booklets is an 8 × 6 twelve-pager offering detailed credits for the complicated collection of music enclosed. This is essentially the box's Rosetta stone, with a summarized version of the credits

comprising the external wrap page that serves as the back cover before the cellophane is removed—helpfully, it's of a trim size that allows it to sit inside the box without folding (often not the case with these things).

Next there's a prism-themed scarf, plus a Lichtenstein-style poster reinterpreting the cover art. A large black envelope contains a reproduction of Roger's handwritten explanation of his idea for the spoken-word text used on the record. In another black envelope are reproductions of a ticket stub and backstage pass, while in a second small

envelope we find four Pink Floyd Collectors' Cards. Then there are nine drink coasters featuring early Storm Thorgerson design sketches proposed for the album, and finally two CDs in card sleeves and a little black velvet bag containing three identical glass marbles portraying the album cover art.

As for the music, a bit frustratingly, the brunt of it is stored deep in the vaults, in other words, carved into the very bottom of the box. That's four of the discs, with two left (as mentioned) to float in card sleeves along with the above goodies. Starting with those, we have Disc 5, a Blu-ray containing "high resolution audio and audio-visual material," much of it represented on the other discs, but here, as noted, upgraded. Disc 6 features a mix of the album plus assorted demos and live material.

Into Discs 1 through 4 as embedded into the box of the album, Disc 1 features the original album, in 2011 remastered form. Disc 2 is the album performed live at Wembley in 1974. Disc 3 is an audio-only DVD, featuring 5.1 Surround, 4.0 Quad, and LPCM Stereo album mixes. Finally, Disc 4 is a proper DVD with 101 minutes of live footage and concert screens, but also a 25-minute documentary on the album, which is as close to liner notes as this box gets.

Again, what you don't get is much of a sense of the first edition of the album, no shot of the original lyric presentation as shown in the gatefold, and neither of the posters or stickers as reproductions (although one of them is pictured in the main booklet). We do, however, get to see small pictures of what the label affixed to the original vinyl looks like as well as a bunch of alternate pyramid shots (and even an alternate sticker). Is this Storm Thorgerson being mischievous? Perhaps it's Storm acting like a true fan, who might complain at getting the same stuff again. Minor complaints aside, the box is plush and fully immersive, especially when it comes to the audio and the visuals, where one could argue that Floyd has given us absolutely everything we would have wanted, stopping short of being repetitive with additional live permutations and the like. How many people have the equipment necessary to make all these mixes of the album come alive is another matter, but if you do, hey, knock yourself out.

Tour Date Archive

Erring on the side of completism, this *Dark Side of the Moon* tour date archive includes three components: 1) 1972 dates, when the songs from the album were performed but it wasn't yet released; 2) 1973 and 1974 dates, which serve as conventional tour dates for the album; and 3) 1975 dates, which, as discussed, serve somewhat as both *Dark Side of the Moon* dates and the only concerts in support of *Wish You Were Here*, which had not been released, but nonetheless was substantially represented. I've excluded the shows with Roland Petit's ballet company in France. This is compiled from multiple sources, with thanks to PinkFloydArchives.com for general structure.

1972

JANUARY
20: The Dome, Brighton, Sussex
21: Guildhall, Portsmouth, Hampshire
22: Winter Gardens, Bournemouth, Hampshire
23: Guildhall, Southampton, Hampshire
27: City Hall, Newcastle-upon-Tyne, Northumberland
28: City Hall, Leeds, Yorkshire

FEBRUARY
3: Locarno Ballroom, Lanchester Polytechnic College, Coventry, Warwickshire
5: Colston Hall, Bristol, Somerset
10: De Montfort Hall, Leicester, Leicestershire
11: Free Trade Hall, Manchester (partial, due to power failure)
12: Sheffield City Hall Oval Hall, Sheffield, Yorkshire
13: Empire Theatre, Liverpool, Lancashire
17–20: Rainbow Theatre, Finsbury Park, London

MARCH
6–7: Tokyo-to Taiikukan, Tokyo, Japan
8–9: Festival Hall, Osaka, Japan
10: Dai-Sho-Gun Furitsu Taiikukan, Kyoto, Japan
13: Nakanoshima Sports Center, Sapporo, Hokkaido, Japan
29–30: Free Trade Hall, Manchester

APRIL
14: Fort Homer Hesterly Armory Auditorium, Tampa, Florida
15: Sportatorium, Hollywood, Florida
16: Township Auditorium, Columbia, South Carolina
18: Symphony Hall, Memorial Arts Center, Atlanta, Georgia
20: Syria Mosque, Pittsburgh, Pennsylvania

21: Lyric Theatre, Baltimore, Maryland
22: Civic Theatre, Akron, Ohio
23: Music Hall, Cincinnati, Ohio
24: Allen Theater, Cleveland, Ohio
26–27: Ford Auditorium, Detroit, Michigan
28: Auditorium Theater, Chicago, Illinois
29: Spectrum, Philadelphia, Pennsylvania

MAY
1–2: Carnegie Hall, New York City, New York
3: Concert Hall, Kennedy Center for Performing Arts, Washington, D.C.
4: Music Hall, Boston, Massachusetts
18: Deutschlandhalle, West Berlin, West Germany
21: Insel Grün, Germersheim, West Germany
22: Olympisch Stadion, Amsterdam, Netherlands

JUNE
28–29: The Dome, Brighton, Sussex

SEPTEMBER
8: Municipal Auditorium, Austin, Texas
9: Music Hall, Houston, Texas
10: McFarlin Auditorium, Southern Methodist University, Dallas, Texas
11: Memorial Hall, Kansas City, Kansas
12: Civic Center, Oklahoma City, Oklahoma
13: Henry Arena, Wichita, Kansas
15: Community Center Arena, Tuscon, Arizona
16: Golden Hall, Community Concourse, San Diego, California
17: Big Surf, Tempe, Arizona
19: Fieldhouse, University of Denver, Denver, Colorado
22: Hollywood Bowl, Los Angeles, California

23–24: Winterland Ballroom, San Francisco, California
27: Vancouver Gardens Arena, Vancouver, British Columbia
28: Memorial Coliseum, Portland, Oregon
29: HEC Edmundson Pavilion, University of Washington, Seattle, Washington
30: Vancouver Gardens Arena, Vancouver, British Columbia

OCTOBER
21: Wembley Empire Pool, London

NOVEMBER
10–11: K.B. Hallen, Copenhagen, Denmark
12: Ernst Merck Halle, Hamburg, West Germany
14: Philips Veranstaltungshalle, Dusseldorf, West Germany
15: Sporthalle, Böblingen, West Germany
16–17: Festhalle, Frankfurt, West Germany
28: Palais des Sports, Toulouse, France
29: Les Arènes, Parc des Expositions, Poitiers, France

DECEMBER
1–2: Centre Sportif l'Île des Vannes, Saint-Ouen, Paris, France
3: Palais des Sports, Caen, France
5: Sport Paleis Vorst National, Brussels, Belgium
7: Palais des Sports, Lille, France
8: Parc des Expositions, Nancy, France
9: Hallenstadion, Zürich, Switzerland
10: Palais des Sports, Lyon, France

1973

MARCH
4: Dane County Memorial Coliseum, Madison, Wisconsin
5: Cobo Hall, Detroit, Michigan
6: Kiel Auditorium, St. Louis, Missouri
7: International Amphitheater, Chicago, Illinois
8: Fieldhouse, University of Cincinnati, Cincinnati, Ohio
10: Memorial Gymnasium, Kent State University, Kent, Ohio
11: Maple Leaf Gardens, Toronto, Ontario
12: The Forum, Montreal, Quebec
14: Music Hall, Boston, Massachusetts
15: The Spectrum, Philadelphia, Pennsylvania
17: Radio City Music Hall, New York City, New York

18: The Palace Theater, Waterbury, Connecticut
19: Civic Center, Providence, Rhode Island
22: Hampton Coliseum, Hampton, Virginia
23: Park Center, Charlotte, North Carolina
24: Municipal Auditorium, Atlanta, Georgia

MAY
18–19: Earls Court Exhibition Hall, Earls Court, London

JUNE
16: Roosevelt Stadium, Jersey City, New Jersey
17: Performing Arts Center, Saratoga, New York
19: Civic Center Arena, Pittsburgh, Pennsylvania
20–21: Merriweather Post Pavilion, Columbia, Maryland
22: Memorial Auditorium, Buffalo, New York
23: Olympia Stadium, Detroit, Michigan
24: Blossom Music Center, Cuyahoga Falls, Ohio
25: Convention Center, Louisville, Kentucky
27: Veterans Memorial Coliseum, Jacksonville, Florida
28: The Sportatorium, Hollywood, Florida
29: Tampa Stadium, Tampa, Florida

OCTOBER
12: Münchener Olympiahalle, Munich, West Germany
13: Stadthalle, Vienna, Austria

NOVEMBER
4: Rainbow Theater, Finsbury Park, London (two shows)

1974

JUNE
18: Hall 1, Palais des Exposition, Toulouse, France
19: Arena, Parc des Expositions, Poitiers, France
21: Palais des Expositions, Dijon, France
22: Théâtre de Plein Air, Parc des Expositions, Colmar, France
24–26: Palais des Sports de la Porte de Versailles, Paris, France

NOVEMBER
4–5: Usher Hall, Edinburgh, Lothian, Scotland
8–9: The Odeon, Newcastle-upon-Tyne, Tyne and Wear
14–17: Empire Pool, Wembley, London
19: Trentham Gardens, Stoke-on-Trent, Staffordshire

22: Sophia Gardens Pavilion, Cardiff, Wales
28–30: Empire Theatre, Liverpool, Lancashire

DECEMBER
3–5: The Hippodrome, Birmingham, West Midlands
9–10: The Palace Theatre, Manchester
13–14: The Hippodrome, Bristol, Avon

1975

APRIL
8: Pacific National Exhibition Park, Vancouver, British Columbia
10: Seattle Center Coliseum, Seattle, Washington
12–13: The Cow Palace, Daly City, California
17: The Coliseum, Denver, Colorado
19: Tucson Community Center Arena, Tuscon, Arizona
20: Activity Center, Arizona State University, Tempe, Arizona
21: Sports Arena, San Diego, California
23–27: Memorial Sports Arena, Los Angeles, California

JUNE
7: Atlanta Stadium, Atlanta, Georgia
9–10: Capital Centre, Landover, Maryland
12–13: The Spectrum, Philadelphia, Pennsylvania
15: Roosevelt Stadium, Jersey City, New Jersey
16–17: Nassau Veterans Memorial Coliseum, Uniondale, New York
18: Boston Garden, Boston, Massachusetts
20: Three Rivers Stadium, Pittsburgh, Pennsylvania
22: County Stadium, Milwaukee, Wisconsin
23–24: Olympia Stadium, Detroit, Michigan
26: Autostade, Montreal, Quebec
28: Ivor Wynne Stadium, Hamilton, Ontario

JULY
5: Knebworth Park, Knebworth, Hertfordshire

A Dark Side Discography

At the moment of writing there were 1,113 iterations of *The Dark Side of the Moon* on Discogs.com, taking into account all formats, territories, and years of issue and reissue. Consider this an extremely selective list of pre-2000 highlights, or more like "milestones" (after that it gets even more complicated, with the theme being sort of everything, everywhere). It gets a little messy with CDs in the early '90s, complicated by inclusions of things in box sets, but then again, the exciting part of the CD story takes place all the way back in 1984.

U.K.

LP Harvest/EMISHVL 8041973

LP Harvest/EMIQ4SHVL 8041973

Cassette Harvest/EMITC-SHVL 8041973

8-Track Harvest/EMI8X-SHVL 8041973

Quad 8-Track Harvest/EMIQ8-SHVL 8041973

Picture disc Harvest/EMISHVL 8041979

CD (made in Japan) Harvest/EMICDP 7 46001 21984

Remastered CD (in *Shine On* box) Harvest/EMIPFBOX 11992

20th Anniversary reissue CD Harvest/EMI0777 7 81479 2 31993

Remastered CD Harvest/EMI7243 8 29752 2 91994

EMI 100th Anniversary edition CD Harvest/EMI7243 8 55673 1 51997

LP Harvest/EMI7243 8 59865 1 21997

U.S.

LP Harvest/Capitol SMAS-11631973

Cassette Harvest/Capitol 4XW-111631973

8-Track Harvest/Capitol 8XW-111631973

Quad 8-Track Harvest/Capitol Q8W-111631973

Picture disc Harvest/Capitol SEAX 119021978

LP Harvest/Mobile Fidelity Sound Lab MFSL 1-10171979

LP Harvest/Mobile Fidelity Sound Lab MFQR 1-0171982

CD (made in Japan) Harvest/Capitol CDP 7 46001 21984

CD Harvest/Mobile Fidelity Sound Lab UDCD 5171988

20th Anniversary reissue CD Harvest/Capitol 0777 7 81479 2 31993

Remastered CD Harvest/Capitol CDP 0777 7 46001 2 51994

Miscellaneous

German LP Harvest/EMI Electrola 1 C 062-05 2491973

French LP Harvest/EMI/Pathe Marconi 2C 064-05.2491973

Canadian LP Harvest/Capitol SMAS-111631973

Australian LP Harvest/EMI SHVLA-8041973

Japanese LP Harvest/EMI/Odeon EOP-807781973

Japanese LP (alternate cover) EMI HW-51491978

Japanese CD Harvest/EMI CP35-30171983

Japanese Collector's Edition CD SQSQ-P001/21998

Image Credits

A = all, B = bottom, L = left, R = right, T = top

Alamy Stock Photo: 8, Pictorial Press; 10TR, Lars Growth; 112TL; 112BL; 113, Neil Baylis; 22T, CBW; 27BR, f8 archive; 28BL, Pictorial Press; 31TR, Pictorial Press; 32, Stefan Wermuth; 35T, Hoo-Me/SMG; 35BR, Hoo-Me/SMG; 37L, Edward Webb; 37R, Gijsbert Hanekroot; 40, Bill Waterson; 42R, Malcolm Park; 45, Katie Collins; 46T, Rolf Adlercreutz; 48, PictureLux; 49R, Gijsbert Hanekroot; 50, PA; 52, Rob Wilkinson; 55B, Art Villone; 72L, Rob Wilkinson; 72B, dcphoto; 73R, Joseph Toth; 84, Pictorial Press; 94, Pictorial Press; 97, Pictorial Press; 99, Media Punch; 103, ZUMA Press; 110, Pictorial Press; 119, Victor Watts; 124, Mirrorpix; 128B, BNA Photographic; 129L, Odile Noel/Lebrecht Music & Arts; 129TR, BA; 133B, Pictorial Press; 136, Media Punch; 138, Media Punch; 140–141, Media Punch; 143, AA Film Archive; 144, Pictorial Press; 147A, Philippe Gras; 152, Media Punch; 160TR, Peter Morgan; 161, Antonio Pagano; 162TL, Rodolfo Sassano; 162TR, Antonio Pagano; 162BL, Sipa USA; 162BR, WENN; 163, Julien De Marchi; 165, World History Archive. **Ann Charters:** 10TL. **Frank White Photo Agency:** 81, 93. **Getty Images:** 11. Andrew Whittuck/Redferns; 15, Michael Ochs Archives; 21, Paul Popper/Popperfoto; 26TL, Gems/Redferns; 35BL, Richard E. Aaron/Redferns; 36, Peter Dazeley; 39, Phil Dent/Redferns; 41, Gijsbert Hanekroot; 43, Jeffrey Mayer/WireImage; 44TL, Nigel Osbourne/Redferns; 54, Chris Morphet, Hulton Archive; 55T, Koh Hasebe/Shinko Music/Hulton Archive; 75, SOPA Images/LightRocket; 76, Koh Hasebe/Shinko Music/Hulton Archive; 78, David Warner Ellis/Redferns; 82, David Warner Ellis/Redferns; 87, Mick Gold/Redferns; 89, DEUTSCH Jean-Claude/Paris Match Archive; 104, Ullstein Bild; 107, Gijsbert Hanekroot; 108, Gijsbert Hanekroot; 112, Gijsbert Hanekroot; 113, Mick Gold/Redferns; 116, Gijsbert Hanekroot; 120, Michael Putland/Hulton Archive; 127, David Warner Ellis/Redferns; 130BR, Jeffrey Mayer/WireImage; 131, Jeffrey Mayer/WireImage; 132, Icon and Image; 135, Michael Ochs Archives; 145, Richard E. Aaron/Redferns; 148TL, Michael Ochs Archives; 148BL, Michael Putland/Hulton Archive; 148TR, Michael Ochs Archives. **Martin Popoff Collection:** 14TR, 19L, 19TR, 20R, 28TL, 29A, 31TL, 51R, 73L, 91, 95, 96, 117, 118, 123T, 126T, 130BL, 133T, 139L, 146, 157, 160TL, 166 –167A. **Motorbooks Archive:** 56–57, 59, 60, 62, 63A, 79, 111, 123B, 125A, 126B, 129BR, 130TK, 134, 139R. **Public Domain:** 10BL, 90. **Robert Alford:** 4, 42TL, 42BL, 51L, 114–115A, 128T, 130TR. **Rock 'n' Roll Comics:** 49L, 122. **Sarah Lee:** 164. **Shutterstock:** 34, cktravels.com. **Soundgas Limited (soundgas.com):** 44BR.

About the Author

At approximately 7,900 (with over 7,000 appearing in his books), Martin Popoff has unofficially written more record reviews than anybody in the history of music writing across all genres. Additionally, Martin has penned approximately 120 books on hard rock, heavy metal, progressive rock, punk, classic rock, and record collecting. He was editor in chief of the now retired *Brave Words & Bloody Knuckles*, Canada's foremost heavy metal publication, for fourteen years, and has contributed to *Revolver, Guitar World, Goldmine, Record Collector,* bravewords.com, lollipop.com, and hardradio.com, with many liner notes to his credit as well. Additionally, Martin has been a regular contractor to Banger Films, having worked for two years as researcher on the award-winning documentary *Rush: Beyond the Lighted Stage,* on the writing and research team for the eleven-episode *Metal Evolution,* and on the ten-episode *Rock Icons,* both for VH1 Classic. Additionally, Martin is the writer of the original heavy metal genre chart used in *Metal: A Headbanger's Journey* and throughout the *Metal Evolution* episodes. He has solo-blabbed all over his own long-running audio podcast, *History in Five Songs with Martin Popoff,* for a number of years, and runs a YouTube channel with his buddy Marco D'Auria called The Contrarians. He is also a guest every Friday morning at 9:00 a.m. on Pete Pardo's Sea of Tranquility YouTube channel. Martin resides in Toronto and can be reached through martinp@inforamp.net or www.martinpopoff.com.

Index

Page numbers in *italic* indicate illustrations